American Academy of Religion Dissertation Series

edited by
H. Ganse Little, Jr.

Number 33

PLURALISM AND TRUTH IN RELIGION
Karl Jaspers on Existential Truth
by
John F. Kane

John F. Kane

Pluralism and Truth in Religion Karl Jaspers on Existential Truth

Scholars Press

Distributed by
Scholars Press
101 Salem Street
Chico, California 95926

PLURALISM AND TRUTH IN RELIGION
Karl Jaspers on Existential Truth

John F. Kane
Ph.D., 1978, McMaster University
Hamilton, Ontario

Library of Congress Cataloging in Publication Data

Kane, John Francis, 1942–
Pluralism and truth in religion.

(Dissertation series—American Academy of Religion ; no. 33)
Originally presented as the author's thesis, McMaster University, 1978.
Bibliography: p.
Includes index.
1. Religion—History. 2. Truth (Theology)—History of Doctrines. 3. Jaspers, Karl, 1883–1969. I. Title II. Series: American Academy of Religion. Dissertation series - American Academy of Religion; no. 33.
BL48.K36 1980 200'.1 80-20659
ISBN 0-89130-413-4
ISBN 0-89130-414-2 (pbk.)

Printed in the United States of America
1 2 3 4 5
Edwards Brothers, Inc.
Ann Arbor, Michigan 48106

TABLE OF CONTENTS

PREFACE

The present study grew, so to speak, from the very atmosphere of a department of religious studies which is devoted quite explicitly to maintaining a pluralistic context for thought about religion. In that atmosphere, where students and faculty encounter other religious traditions not only in books but in the person of their colleagues, questions about religious truth have gained a certain legitimacy, even though they are still far too often excluded by the dominant mode of historical scholarship.

The specific impetus for this study came from Harry Wardlaw, Professor of Philosophical Theology at the Melbourne College of Divinity, who first introduced me to Jaspers during the 1971-72 academic year when he served as visiting professor at McMaster University. It was Harry who made introductions to Professor Fritz Buri and helped with arrangements for a delightful spring and summer at the Theologische Fakultät in Basel. Buri's enthusiasm for the project, his long familiarity with Jaspers' work, and his personal involvement in inter-religious dialogue provided a context of cheerful and critical support during that period of research at the university where Jaspers spent the final third of his academic life.

Specific acknowledgement of those at McMaster who helped me during the course of this study is difficult because the list of both faculty and fellow students is so long. I must begin with Ian Weeks who, as instructor, supervisor, and friend, knew not only how to ask the right questions, but how to let the answers grow on their own terms, in the logic of the life lived. As past and present dissertation committee members, John Robertson, Louie Greenspan, Wayne Whillier, and Gary Madison all took the time to read, question, criticize, and generally to prod me to more clearheaded and careful thinking. Dr. George Grant helped me, in ways he will never know, to take that thinking seriously. Gerard Vallée, David Ard, Kassie Temple, Koichi Shinohara, Bob Gilliam, Paul Younger, Gene Combs, Joe Kroger,

Art Davis--these are some of those who, whether over a book or a beer, contributed to that atmosphere or life of thought whence the specific concerns of the present work grew.

Jeanie Demmler, of course, deserves special mention. I am continually assisted by her sociological penchant for concrete facts and empirical data. Yet it was and remains the lived particularity and passion of her faith which has made life together that deeper and richer dialogue which is the real subject of this study.

Finally I want to thank Marsha Callahan for her patient, cheerful, and generous work preparing the typed manuscript.

Some Notes on References and Translations:

(1) For the sake of convenience Jaspers' works are referred to in what follows either by title alone or by abbreviations (in the case of book-length and frequently cited works). Complete bibliographic information along with a listing of all abbreviations is given in the Bibliography.

(2) Where foreign language sources are cited, the translation is my own unless otherwise indicated.

(3) Since Jaspers has, in general, been well served by his major English translators, I have not hesitated to use their translations even though I have checked them against the original whenever I thought it necessary. My only change in these translations has been my use throughout, for reasons of consistency, of "encompassing" to translate *umgreifend*.

(4) When translating from German I have not capitalized abstract nouns like "being" or "spirit" or "transcendence." There is no grammatical warrant for such capitalization and it actually falsifies Jaspers' sense. I have, however, left such capitalization as appears in other translations.

(5) Following the practice of Jaspers' translators, I have not translated "Existenz" and have not treated it as a foreign word. I have taken it over into English, just as Jaspers took it over into German from Kierkegaard's Danish.

J. F. K.

McMaster University
April 1978

I
INTRODUCTION

In simplest terms, this thesis is an analysis and critique of Karl Jaspers' discussion of one of the central problems facing contemporary religious thought--the problem of religious truth as it arises within contemporary consciousness of religious pluralism. Specifically, it looks at Jaspers' affirmative answer to the question, "Can more than one religion be true?", and seeks to determine the adequacy of the idea of truth whereby Jaspers explains such a possibility. It is, then, an analysis of Jaspers' idea of "existential truth" or, more exactly, of his use of that idea in explaining religious truth in a situation of religious pluralism. While finding Jaspers' thought influential and important, the thesis concludes that it is finally inadequate, and develops a series of related criticisms explaining this inadequacy--criticisms which simultaneously point toward other ways of approaching the question of religious truth which might be more adequate to the reality of religious pluralism.

In this introductory chapter (1) a brief and general discussion of what is meant by the problem of pluralism and truth in religion will be followed by (2) introductory remarks about Jaspers, especially as regards the rationale for choosing to study his thought on the topic of religious pluralism and truth. These first sections lead to (3) a preliminary statement of the thesis to be argued, and thus of both the goals and limitations of this study. Finally, (4) a brief methodological discussion of the way in which Jaspers' thought will be approached will be followed by a concluding outline of the structure or movement of the discussion in subseqent chapters.

1.

It is a commonplace of everyday experience as well as of learned comment that there is today little consensus and less clarity concerning religious truth.[1] For those of us who live in the modern, secular, post-religious West,[2] any reference to "the problem of religious truth" actually entails a complex tangle of different but related problems.

In a most general sense, religious truth is problematic insofar as perhaps the most characteristic attitude concerning it is one of practical indifference. A general climate of skeptical relativism which dichotomizes facts and values, restricting the latter to the sphere of privacy, creates a situation where even for the believer judgments of religious truth are often indistinguishable from matters of taste or opinion--except, of course, during those historical episodes when they erupt into the public realm in the form of ideological frenzy. The situation has been well described by the theologian Karl Rahner in response to the question "What does the average European of today feel about religious truth?"--except that his reply is pertinent not only to "the average European."

> His attitude might perhaps be described as follows. Apart from the simple facts of direct sense experience which can be verified anew at any time by experiment, there are theories and opinions and nothing else.... Knowledge of truth, to the extent, that is, that it is constituted by a definite content has, therefore, moved from the center of human existence to its periphery. It belongs with things like color of hair, taste, race, on which man's absolute value cannot be made to depend.[3]

In such a pervasive climate of practical skepticism there are, as already stated, a whole range of specific issues or problems concerning religious truth. Yet what is perhaps most significant is a general shift in the ground of debate about religious truth. Thus the fundamental questions are no longer primarily questions of fact--questions about this or that religious truth, about the truth of this or that religion, or even about whether the claims of any religion are true. Such traditional questions about the truth or falsity of religious claims are, to be sure, still prevalent. But the more fundamental questions have to do with whether or not it is at all appropriate to understand religions in terms of truth--and if it is, then how is such truth to be understood? They are, then, not *factual* questions about whether this or that is true, but *logical* questions about the very idea of "religious truth."

Thus, to take but two examples from recent discussions about religion, the famous (or infamous) *University* debate on

"Theology and Falsification" and recent discussions about religion and science both exemplify the shift in philosophical thought about religion from the question of factual truth to the question about the meaning or logical status of religious truth claims. The *University* debate[4] turned upon the question of whether religious assertions make any sense *as assertions*, as statements which could be judged true or false. Or are they cognitively meaningless and thus not properly matters of truth (at least of religious truth) at all?

Similarly, recent discussion about religion and science,[5] discussion in large measure prompted by the type of attack on religious belief found in the "Theology and Falsification" debate, illustrates both this shift in the focus of philosophical concern about religion and the logically problematic status of the idea of religious truth. In response to the accusation of cognitive meaninglessness, the effort has been made to ground cognitive significance by showing the logical similarities between religion and science. Yet the difference between scientific truth and religious truth implied in these efforts is revealing. For while there are not only continual (factual) disagreements about scientific truths, but also (logical) disagreements about the meaning of "scientific truth," there are no such disagreements about whether it is appropriate to speak of truth in matters of science. It is, in fact, precisely because there is general agreement *that* science is a matter of truth (and because science is often taken as *the* paradigm instance of the very idea of truth), that efforts to establish the appropriateness of speaking of religious truth have turned to comparisons between the logic of religion and the logic of science. The necessity for such efforts serves to underscore the difference between science and religion. While efforts to understand the idea of truth in science stem from the presupposition of that truth, similar efforts to understand the logic of religious truth claims are, in fact, finally concerned to establish the legitimacy of speaking about "religious truth."

Now among the many specific issues involved in and illustrative of the generally problematic character of the idea of religious truth, one particular issue of major contemporary significance is the problem of pluralism and truth, or the problem emerging from the apparently conflicting truth claims of the various world religions. As John Hick notes in a new chapter devoted to this problem in the most recent edition of his *Philosophy of Religion*, "this issue now emerges as a major topic demanding a prominent place on the agenda of the philosopher of religion today and in the future."[6] It is a problem which is increasingly actual or pressing--both for those religious persons engaged in the dialogue of religions[7] and for those engaged in reflective analysis of religion.[8] It is, moreover, an issue which brings the problematic logical status of religious truth into particularly sharp focus. As John Hick notes in the passage just cited, "the skeptical thrust of these questions goes very deep; for it is a short step from the thought that the different religions cannot all be true, although they each claim to be, to the thought that in all probability none of them is true."[9] And it can be said with equal justice, to paraphrase Hick, that it is but a short step from the frequently voiced claim that all of the great religions are in some sense true to a perplexing problem about the propriety and meaning of the word "true" being used here.

People have always, of course, been aware of the fact that there were many religions, and there have always been some who took seriously the truth claims of other religions. Yet a general awareness of the historically changing and culturally specific character of particular religions (including one's own), along with a more widespread appreciation of the richness and plausibility of other religions, is a more modern phenomenon. It is, moreover, this new or heightened awareness, itself born of a new world-historical situation, which has generated the particular issue with which this study is concerned.[10]

The new world situation has been described and explained in many ways. Whether greeted optimistically as "a global village" or anticipated with trepidation as "a brave new world," the advent of a potentially universal and homogeneous world culture under the impetus of modern scientific and industrial technique has been recognized as our new spiritual situation at least since Hegel. Increasingly the spread of technical rationality along the trading routes and (more recently) the airwaves of the world has penetrated the previously secure boundaries of particular, traditional cultures. It has simultaneously brought these cultures into protracted, demanding contact with one another and, perhaps more significantly, with the emergent, largely alien, yet inescapable presence of modern industrial civilization.

The resulting--and, of course, still emerging--situation for the religions is first of all a situation of varying degrees of *crisis* (or at least of radical change) brought about by the diminution of the particular, traditional culture in which a given religion's pattern of life and self-understanding was rooted[11] and by the necessity, again in varying degrees, of adapting to the new (secular) cultural situation.[12] Secondly, it is a situation of new and more sustained contact between the world religions and, as so often noted, of an actual or potential *convergence* of the religions.

One way of characterizing this new situation of encounter between the religions would be to say that it is no longer simply a matter of a primarily "academic" comparison of doctrines and data, but has become a meeting of persons. As Wilfred Smith remarks, "the large-scale compilation of data of the nineteenth century...has in the twentieth century and particularly since World War II been supplemented by a living encounter--a large-scale face-to-face meeting between persons of diverse faith."[13] The new awareness of other religions emerging in this situation, then, is not simply a matter of knowledge, but more significantly a matter of growing respect, appreciation, and mutual influence--and this during a period of increasing self-criticism and loss of confidence resulting from the first-mentioned crisis aspect of the new world-situation.

Yet this new or heightened consciousness of religious pluralism which is characteristic of our situation is not without complexity and ambiguity. It is, in fact, deeply problematic, although in some respects its problems are also quite significant opportunities. For many, of course, it is understood as simply one aspect of that general sense of relativism which renders the whole idea of truth peripheral. For others--those for whom it represents a serious encounter of persons and living faiths, characterized by openness and appreciation--it is a consciousness troubled by serious, often unprecedented questions precisely as a result of this new-found appreciation of the plausibility of the other *as other*.

For some, of course, this awareness of pluralism raises the type of questions traditionally dealt with in the philosophy of religion (or philosophical theology)--questions about the validity of any religion or about general truths which may be shared by several religions (e.g., that God or Divine Being exists; that miracle and revelation are possible). There are, too, especially for many Western Christians, theological questions--not simply the old questions about how "the others" can be saved, but questions about how other religions as religions are to be understood and appreciated within the framework of one's own faith.[14] For many thoughtful persons, however, the pressing questions emerging from a heightened awareness of pluralism are neither strictly theological (since they do not presuppose the normative truth of any one tradition) nor the traditional philosophical questions (since they do presuppose that religion in some general sense is true or that there is religious truth). Their questions center, rather, on the adequacy of the widespread view, expressed variously and held with varying degrees of explicitness, that more than one religion is true or that all of the great religions are true, each in its own way as a symbolic, culturally and historically specific articulation of the inexpressible divine mystery. This last question is the specific concern of the present study.[15]

Quite typically, at least in the West, such a view about different religions being equally true, along with the doubts and questions associated with it, might arise in something like the following pattern of thought. The heightened awareness of pluralism resulting both from a growing appreciation of the other as other and an increasingly critical appropriation of one's own faith has made suspect, for many, the claim of any one religion to full or normative truth precisely by giving a certain legitimacy to many other claims. Thus, for example, Christian exclusivism is attacked from within. Recent efforts to develop a "theology of religions" are dismissed as insufficiently radical, as so many epicycles of theory used to shore up a failing Ptolemaic (Christocentric) theology when what is really needed is a Copernican revolution.[16] After such a revolution, "there will not be Christian theologies, or Islamic theologies...but human theologies, which are not sectional but global in their use of the religious data...theologies based upon the full range of man's religious awareness."[17] A different, and far more modest example, would be the recent critique of so much phenomenology of religion because it effectively, whether explicitly or only implicitly, uses only one religion (Christianity) as normative.[18]

At the same time, however, assertions about the essential unity of the religions, their unitive origins and fundamental agreement ("they all really teach the same thing") are found wanting. Detailed scholarly work in the history of religions has shown such facile assertions of unity to be without basis. Differences among the religions, for example, which were regarded as secondary by earlier theories about the origins of religion, have been shown to be as basic or original as similarities.[19] And it is the same with regard to the subsequent histories and current expressions of belief and practice.

> It is clear enough that there are structural similarities running through all the major religions...and that there are analogies among their doctrines, sometimes even striking analogies. But adding up all the similarities and analogies we can find among them seems to leave us far short of the evidence needed to warrant the claim that they are saying the same thing.[20]

If we take the religions at their word, "if we go by the words enshrining their beliefs," we not only find no evidence for unanimity, but rather that "there are different teachings"--real opposition, conflicting claims.[21]

Thus a "loose and sentimental"[22] view of the oneness of the religions seems no more adequate than the orthodox assertion of normative truth. Neither traditional "provincialism" nor a more modern "cosmopolitanism" seems to come to grips with the actual dimensions of the problem of pluralism and truth as it presses itself upon this contemporary consciousness.[23] To the extent that some continue to affirm that their religion is the true religion, their "provincialism" is troubled by their awareness of and respect for the other religions *as other* and not simply as a preliminary or partial form of their own truth. To the extent that the experiences of others has led them to reject "provincial" claims, their "cosmopolitanism" is equally troubled by the fact that their truth bears strangely little resemblance to any actual religion (to the actual claims of the religions) and is divorced from the concrete life and practice so essential to the actual religions.[24]

What can be neatly formulated as a seemingly straightforward alternative, then, has become in the actual experience of many an extremely complex dilemma. If one is to speak of religious truth in the context of pluralism, then it can be *said* quite simply that either one religion is true (and all others either false or only partially true) or that something like "Religion" is true (and religions are true insofar as they embody or manifest this essence--insofar as they all "say the same thing"). Yet it is precisely the unacceptability of either alternative which constitutes the dilemma and which has led to the suggestion of a third possibility as an escape from the dilemma. If no one religion may be said to embody, in a final and normative way, the fullness of religious truth, and if it is inadequate to find the truth of religion in some hypothetical essence of religion or religion-in-general, then perhaps more than one religion may be said to be true. In other words, given the problems posed by the modern awareness of religious pluralism, it is, perhaps, only in terms of a view which admits the possibility that more than one religion can be true--or that irreducibly different religions may be equally true--that the sense and legitimacy of assertions of religious truth can be maintained.

Such in any case is the type of view which has attained fairly wide currency because of its obvious attractiveness for a heightened, modern awareness of pluralism. If "the reality of pluralism must be the starting point of any serious modern faith,"[25] then the assertion that more than one religion could be true would safeguard religious particularity and particular claims, allowing equal weight to pluralism and to truth. This type of view is, of course, not new. It might be said to go back at least to Friedrich Schleiermacher, to whose influence so much in the contemporary study of and understanding of religion can be traced.[26] Yet if it is not new, it has become increasingly prominent because it seems to meet the problematic demands of the type of awareness of pluralism described above.[27]

For many today, then, the notion that different religions might be equally true is a promising and extremely attractive one. Yet its attraction should perhaps be described as seductive, as a "bewitchment of intelligence." For while all aspects of contemporary consciousness of religious pluralism raise serious problems for claims to religious truth, the line of thinking just summarized raises with particular acuteness basic logical questions about the meaning of "religious truth." Surely it is generally held, as a critic of the view that "all religions are equally true" stresses, that "what is really true for us must be universally true, for that is what truth means."[28] Thus if it is claimed that more than one religion can, strictly speaking, be said to be true, it must be explained what the word "true" means in such a context, lest it be reduced to some merely private sense like "I choose this" or "I approve of this."[29] Put negatively, the problem is whether the view that different, conflicting truth claims can be equally true does not render the very idea of religious truth vacuous. Put more positively, the problem is to determine whether it is possible to understand religious truth in a way which at once respects the particularity of the different traditions and still gives substance to the idea of truth.

There are, of course, various efforts to arrive at just such an understanding of religious truth. These different efforts, moreover, tend to overlap at key points and to share various aspects of a common type of approach to religious pluralism and truth. Still, while an examination of the adequacy of this increasingly widespread way of thinking is the general purpose of this study, no attempt shall be made here to survey a variety of different theories or to distill the major elements of a supposedly common theory. What is proposed, rather, is more modest: a partial assessment of the view that more than one religion could be true by means of an analysis of the explanatory theory developed by one major and significant proponent of that view--Karl Jaspers. To put the matter another way: the question with which this study is concerned is not the factual one, "Is there more than one true religion?", but the logical or critical question, "Can there be more than one true religion?" Even more precisely, the question takes the following form: "Can truth in religion be (adequately) understood in such a way that more than one religion can be true--even when there is clear opposition in the fundamental truth claims made by the different religions?" Jaspers' thought is examined as a major contemporary example of an affirmative answer to that question.

Before turning to some introductory comments about Jaspers, however, two more points should be made about the problem area which has just been sketched out. In the first place, and for the sake of clarity, it should be emphasized again that the precise problem under study is only one limited aspect of the general problem of pluralism and truth (which is itself only one of many problems related to the generally problematic character of religious truth). The general problem or context of problems raised by contemporary awareness of religious pluralism has been touched upon both because it constitutes a constant horizon within which thought about the precise problem occurs and because increased clarity about the more precise issues becomes one way of dealing with and making some contribution toward the resolution of the larger issues. Still, while there is such an implicit intention or direction of thought throughout the present study, the explicit focus is limited to Jaspers' thought as one example of a prevalent type of thinking and also to the critical or logical questions which remain preliminary to what must finally be the more significant questions--those questions about the actual validity of different religious claims which emerge in the convergence or encounter of the religions themselves.[30]

Secondly, however, while the explicit focus is thus limited and logical, the question under discussion is no narrowly academic quibble. As thinkers of the stature of Kierkegaard and Nietzsche have taught us, and as Jaspers himself stresses,[31] the question of the meaning, and thus of the very possibility of religious truth is a matter of "political" significance in the most profound sense of that word. The continuing privatization of religious truth and the corresponding paralysis of the great traditions of belief are matters touching the depth and future of our humanity. His awareness of this political seriousness is, in fact, prominent among the reasons why Jaspers is taken to be a major and significant representative of the general approach to religious pluralism and truth being considered here.

2.

There are, of course, various reasons for the selection of Jaspers' discussion of religious pluralism and truth as the focus of this study. The most straightforward reason is the simple fact that he has written a major work which deals with the precise problem outlined above--*Der philosophische Glaube angesichts der Offenbarung*--and that his claim to have provided an adequate resolution to this problem has yet to receive a detailed analysis and evaluation.[32] The more serious reason, of course, is found in the view expressed above that Jaspers is a major representative of the type of thinking about pluralism and truth which has just been sketched in broad outline.[33] There can be no argument to prove this estimate of Jaspers' significance, but a brief introduction to his discussion of religious pluralism will serve to illustrate some of the ways in which he is, in the best sense, typical and representative. Such an introduction is perhaps particularly useful in North America where Jaspers is known above all simply as "an existentialist," a title which probably conceals more than it reveals and one which he explicitly rejected,[34] and where he is known hardly at all for the thinking about religion which became a major concern of his later years and about which, as already noted, there has been much discussion in Europe.[35]

It is in a way ironic that Jaspers is not more widely known particularly for his understanding of religion since he speaks so persuasively not only to but also for a liberal, enlightened, yet troubled mainstream of thinking about religion. German theologian Heinrich Fries' testimony in this regard remains substantially true today, a quarter of a century after it was written:

> If according to Hegel's famous phrase an authentic philosophy is nothing other than "the era grasped conceptually," then this is especially applicable to Jaspers and his work. This philosopher and his philosophy express for many who cannot give expression to their thought that which is alive in them as the spirit of the age. Thus is the figure and the work of Jaspers representative: he both presents

> and represents what is thought and lived today. In meeting Jaspers, we meet the man of our day.[36]

Yet Jaspers is not more widely known for his thinking about religion in part, at least, because of his own initial and continuing intention to speak about and for philosophy as an original faith distinct from and in polar opposition to religious faith. Jaspers never claimed to be religious in any generally accepted sense. From his youth until the very end of his life he maintained a simultaneously critical and respectful distance from institutional Christianity, even as he was deeply influenced by the heritage of "biblical religion" made present to some extent by his own family, but to a greater extent by his Jewish wife and by his own personal study.[37] His early writing about religion focuses upon religion primarily in order to distinguish philosophy from religion.[38] Only in his later work does religion itself become a topic of thought and concern where Jaspers seeks "to promote truth in religion by means of a philosophical critique of religion."[39] It is in this later work, both as part of his effort to develop a "philosophical logic" adequate to the new, world-historical situation (or global horizon) of thought and as part of his passionate struggle to preserve the possibility of faith amidst the terrible crisis of our age, that Jaspers takes up the question of pluralism and truth in religion.[40]

Thus Jaspers' relation to religious faith is one which grew gradually throughout his career as he again and again took up the struggle to come to adequate terms with that other faith which stood in such a crucial polarity to his own "philosophical faith." Yet while there clearly is development in Jaspers' understanding of religion,[41] the controlling elements and basic intentions of his thought remain constant. Even as he contrasts philosophy and religion in the early work, his fundamental purpose is to establish the validity of existential faith (or the truth of existential relations to transcendence). Philosophy clearly is the primary path of such existential transcending, but Jaspers, with all of his severe criticism of religion, stresses that it too is a possible path, faith, and truth.[42] Later, as his thinking became more world-historical and political,[43] this fundamental intention to establish the validity of existential faith takes the form of an effort to delineate a "universal basic knowledge" as a "common framework so broadly based that historically heterogeneous faiths could communicate in it without abandoning themselves" and "could transform themselves by their own depth...into the new foundations that human seriousness needs under the conditions of the coming age."[44] Thus the truth of faith might survive the pervasive threat of decay into nihilism, the loss of the great religious and philosophical traditions, by the establishment of a basis upon which these traditions might be affirmed in their multiplicity--for "the truth of faith lies in the multiplicity of its historical manifestations" and "in the self-encountering of this multiplicity through ever deeper communication."[45] This basis for the affirmation of the plurality of faiths, for their possible preservation in a situation of crisis and for their communication in a situation of convergence, is constituted by Jaspers' analysis of the logic of faith and the logic of existential truth.

In sum, then, a distinction can and must be made between Jaspers' faith and his analysis of faith. Jaspers' "philosophical faith," however religious it might seem in its unconditionality and transcendent reference, must clearly be distinguished from the positivity of real religion.[46] This non-religious faith is itself very widespread and typical of the faith of so many contemporaries who stand with Jaspers between a complete rejection of faith, on the one hand, and traditional orthodoxy, on the other.[47] Yet it is Jaspers' analysis of faith, intended to be applicable to religious as well as philosophical faith, which is typical of contemporary thinking about religion in a more fundamental sense. It is this analysis of the logic of faith and truth which crystallized in Jaspers' own thinking in light of the present situation of crisis and convergence and which is taken here as representative of not just a-religious, but also of much religious self-understanding as it has developed in that same situation.

Jaspers' thinking is intentionally typical not simply in the sense already noted that he seeks a common framework adequate to the problems and realities of our age, but insofar as he seeks that common ground not by some radical breakthrough or new departure, but by a self-conscious effort to think within and to recapitulate the dominant themes of Western and contemporary thinking. "I see in my thinking," he notes with reference to the "universal basic knowledge" (*Grundgedanke*) outlined in the first part of *Von der Wahrheit*, "the natural and necessary conclusion of previous Western thought."[48] Jaspers has always rejected the idea that his philosophy is something new. "Philosophy can never wish to be anything but simple, ancient, eternal philosophy."[49] Yet this effort to be ancient, eternal philosophy occurs today explicitly within the conditions for thought which are the realities of our era and not by some effort to transcend those conditions. Thus Jaspers locates himself clearly and self-consciously within, as one of the most significant representatives of, the modern, enlightened tradition of liberal rationality. Kant stands at the peak of that tradition as the one who most clearly thought the fundamental conditions of our age. And it is above all Kant who is Jaspers' mentor and a Kantian understanding of reason and freedom which are the foundations of his thinking.[50]

Yet the heritage of the Enlightenment has undergone a deep challenge and crisis since the middle of the last century--so much so that Karl Löwith can with justice remark that "we are all existentialists...because we are all more or less caught in the predicament of being 'modern' by living in an epoch of dissolution of former beliefs and certainties."[51] Here again, or still, it is Jaspers' concern to think within and not against the mainstream of the age--to think the Western tradition as appropriated by the Enlightenment within the present crisis of our history. Kant remains his mentor, but his is a Kantian thinking drawn taut under the impact of Nietzsche and sharpened by the influence of Kierkegaard. Reason and freedom (*Vernunft und Existenz*) remain the focal points of his thought--as they are the dominant realities of our historical situation--but it is reason and freedom chastened by the loss of secure foundations, rootlessness, the ambiguities of scientific technique, and the unclear prospect of the emerging global era.[52]

Jaspers has always, then, sought to think in a way which was representative of the mainstream--not as a passive mirror of the superficial, but as one who grappled with and thus clarified the deeper currents. This is equally true for his thinking about religion, both for his general analysis of the logic of faith and for his specific approach to the question of religious pluralism. The fundamental elements of that analysis of the logic and truth of faith reveal the pervasive presence of Kant and Kierkegaard and thus find echoes throughout very much current discussion of religion. Emphasis upon faith with an implied priority of faith over belief and the basic location of religion in subjectivity or immediacy is itself a prime instance of understanding religion within Kant's anthropocentric turn and in terms of Kierkegaard's evocation of *Existenz*. Similarly Kant's programmatic denial of knowledge "to make room for faith" establishes a polarity of phenomenal and noumenal, objective and transcendent, literal and symbolic which finds comprehensive contemporary expression in Jaspers' thought and is an often unquestioned and seemingly inescapable premise of so much recent discussion of religion.

Jaspers, then, brings these fundamental aspects of his analysis of faith to the current situation of crisis and convergence and provides thereby one of the clearer and more comprehensively thought expressions of the view that the truth of faith allows, even demands real plurality.[53] Already in 1931, writing about the plurality of world views in the history of human thought, he described the basic problem raised by such pluralism--what has above been described as the dilemma of "provincialism" or "cosmopolitanism":

> It seems that there is either one true way or the truth is the combination that links them all, *or else there are several truths*. If there were many exclusive world views and all of them were true, the *applicable truth concept would have to differ from what we mean by generally valid scientific truth*.[54]

Given such alternatives, Jaspers vigorously rejects the orthodox or "provincial" claim ("one true way"). It is, in fact, the exclusivist pretensions of revealed religion which eventually came to occupy a central place in his critique of religion.[55] Yet Jaspers is equally clear in his rejection of some "cosmopolitan" essence or amalgam of the various religious faiths ("the combination that links them all"). Past efforts to find the one truth in the diversity of religions have resulted not in "authentic truth purified of historical accident" but in "a collection of abstractions watered down by rationalism" where "the profound meaning, the poignancy was lost" and "trivial generalization remained."[56] The remaining alternative, then, is that more than one religion can be true ("there are several truths"), but this, as Jaspers notes, means that "the applicable truth concept would have to differ from what we mean by generally valid scientific truth." It would be a concept of "existential truth" which, while unconditional and absolute, remains always particular and historic, never universal and exclusive.[57]

Jaspers' program, then, laid out early in his career and followed consistently throughout the different shifts and developments of his thinking, is to argue for the pervasive type of response to pluralism which admits plurality in its understanding of truth. His constant goal has been to clarify a common framework of thinking expressive of the deepest currents of our heritage and present situation, a framework which would make possible the survival of multiple faiths in toleration, communication, and truth. Not only has this goal been central to Jaspers' thinking, but that thinking itself has always sought to be as comprehensive as possible--in the sense of comprehensively open to other faiths and ways of thinking and, perhaps more significantly, in the sense of a systematic or comprehensive effort to think through his position from foundations to implications. Thus a particular advantage of focusing on Jaspers' discussion of pluralism and truth, and a particular merit of that discussion, is its comprehensive character. Here is no merely technical or academic discussion in the philosophy of religion, but a discussion which is central to a comprehensively-thought philosophy,[58] a philosophy which itself seeks to grapple comprehensively with the central issues and ideas of our day.

While there are many today who would maintain that different religions can be equally true because religious truth is unlike scientific truth, because it is a matter of "faith" and its articulations are "symbolic," there are few who have *argued* that position by a serious analysis of the logic of religious truth and a systematic grounding of that logic in firm philosophical foundations. And there are fewer yet for whom that argument is part of a serious, inescapably political engagement with the destiny of our humanity in this age of crisis.[59] This is not, of course, to say that Jaspers is unique nor even to claim that his analysis of religious pluralism is necessarily the best or the most profound. Yet it at least lends plausibility to the claim that Jaspers' clarification of the truth of faith could be of "pervasive consequence."[60] It is this plausibility which will be evaluated in what follows.

There is, however, one final note which should be included in this brief introduction to Jaspers' discussion of religious pluralism. In his intention to speak to and for a (the?) mainstream of contemporary thinking, and in his effort to grapple with the deeper currents of our age, Jaspers comes to be representative not only of the good, but also, inevitably, of some of the central problems and conflicts of this troubled age. Moreover, the effort to think comprehensively leads not to an avoidance or veiling of those problems, but to even greater clarification. Said another way, Jaspers' thinking does not avoid the difficulties nor does it ignore the limitations of the present situation of thought. Rather it consciously reflects these difficulties as well as the ambiguities, unresolved questions, and darkness which sometimes result when the best efforts of thought fall short before them. Thus it simultaneously (and self-consciously) argues for a particular understanding of religious pluralism and truth while inviting, even provoking, a critical but communicative response to that understanding.[61]

3.

To repeat, then, what has been said above about the limited, specific goal of the present study--it is to engage in just such critical struggle with Jaspers' thinking as a way of assessing one major and representative instance of the view that more than one religion can be true. Because of the difficulty of the issue and the complexity of the thinker, it should not be surprising that a mixed verdict is reached. There is much in Jaspers' thought that recommends itself as adequate for understanding religious truth and for coming to grips with the reality of religious pluralism. But there are also inadequacies in particularly crucial aspects of his analysis. In sum, then, the thesis to be defended maintains a tentatively negative answer to the basic question about the possibility of more than one religion being true. At least in terms of Jaspers' exposition, it is argued that such a possibility has not been adequately established.

When seen primarily as an evaluation of Jaspers' thought, this thesis argues that he fails because of a deep ambiguity or tension in his position--insofar as key aspects of his analysis betray or undercut the explicit intention of his argument--and because his analysis of the logic of faith, despite much that is helpful, falls short of an adequate understanding of religious reality and truth. Yet his failure is instructive insofar as it illustrates the way in which certain widespread ways of thinking about religion are not only problematic in themselves, but pervert or derail much else that is valuable in that same contemporary appreciation of religion and religious pluralism. When seen, then, as a particular and limited effort to deal with the question of religious truth as it arises in the contemporary situation of pluralism, this thesis argues that the widely held view that more than one religion can be true has serious difficulties insofar as it is explained by the type of thinking found in Jaspers. This view is not established by that type of thinking.

Yet it bears reiteration that this thesis certainly does not provide any final resolution to the general problem of pluralism and truth. Nor does it resolve the specific logical issue which is its particular focus. It argues that a particular way of understanding religious truth is inadequate, but there may yet be more adequate understandings of religious truth which do admit of significant plurality. Furthermore, this thesis does not claim to offer a complete analysis of Jaspers' philosophy. It is not primarily an argument about the full scope of his idea of existential truth nor an evaluation of his total thought about religion--although both topics figure heavily in the discussion. It is, rather, simply an attempt to get to the heart of Jaspers' thinking about religious pluralism in order to determine whether that thinking provides a basis for affirming a possible plurality of true religions.

4.

There is, however, one more issue which must be at least touched upon in this introductory chapter, an issue which is raised by the intention to "get to the heart of Jaspers' thinking" on a particular issue. The corpus of Jaspers' work is, simply in terms of size, so massive, with so many different texts and themes bearing on the topic of religious truth, that any attempt at "getting to the heart of the matter" would seem, at least at first glance, to raise methodological difficulties.[62] Those difficulties, moreover, would seem to be significantly increased by particular aspects of Jaspers' style which reflect his own quite deliberate methodology and which render attempts at neat summarization not only impossible, but very wrong-headed. The following are some examples of that style developed by Jaspers in his search for an adequate form for written philosophical communication.[63]

> Using a language which, in the words of his major translator, "fits the principle of inconclusiveness," Jaspers stresses "primordial words" (such as "idea," "mind," "world," and "ground") which are "incapable of objective definition" and he leaves almost nothing unqualified by "a stream of meticulous and-yets, whereases, and on-the-other-hands."[64]
>
> He deliberately avoids a rigid set of technical terms. In his own words: "I take great care to avoid too much terminological precision. Clarity is attained by the movement of thought not by the definition of concepts."[65]
>
> Clarity does not preclude deliberate ambiguity and unresolved (unresolvable) dialectic where truth demands them. Thus Jaspers' thinking continually moves across the hyphen between both-and, simultaneously asserting "yes" and "no" and refusing an illusory finality or synthesis.[66]
>
> The organization of his works is designedly fluid and open. It allows for continual circling, a repetition or re-introduction of themes and ideas in different contexts and combinations. There is a pervasive unity, but it is not a typical beginning-middle-end, neatly logical unity. It is more like the movement of a river as it twists and even turns back upon itself, receives new impulses, now fast now gentle, but grows as a whole in depth and power.[67]

> While his thinking seeks to present a comprehensive framework for contemporary thought and faith, and while it is certainly systematic (thorough and interconnected), it programmatically rejects the possibility of a rigid, complete "System." [68] The parts of the whole, while in basic harmony, are not cogs which fit neatly together. They are, rather, each by itself, reflections on a particular issue or topic, movements of thought which attain a relative completeness.[69]

There can be, then, no adequate summary of Jaspers' thought[70] because, as he insists repeatedly, living philosophy is not a set of doctrines, but a movement of thinking. Ideas, thought structures, and teachings are necessary, "but the point of reference lies not in the doctrine itself, but in the possible goal of the motion."[71] It is not, cannot be a fixed or final set of doctrines because the "possible goal of the motion" is, as we shall see, ever-ungraspable transcendence. The purpose of philosophical communication, then, is the communication of a movement of thinking, a communication which is possible only insofar as it enables the reader/hearer to enter into the movement itself. In Jaspers' striking metaphor, that personal ("existential") participation is like "the beating of the other wing without which the contents of the text--the beating of the first wing--cannot bring about the upswing of fulfilled meaning."[72] "Philosophical truth," in other words, "can be communicated only in indirect thought-movements and cannot adequately be captured in any proposition."[73] It is the purpose of Jaspers' stylistic or methodological peculiarities to effect such indirect communication, to stimulate or involve that movement of thinking even as they frustrate the ever-present desire for a fixed, secure system or doctrine by leaving the contents of thought ever "in suspension" (*Schwebend*).[74]

Thus while there must be fidelity to Jaspers' text, a simple material reproduction or attempted summary of the text will not "go to the heart" of his thinking. If more than such external reproduction is necessary for the interpretation of any thinker of stature, it is doubly necessary for someone (like Jaspers) who programmatically or methodically distinguishes the conceptual apparatus from the intended movement of thought.[75] The alternative to merely external reproduction is the effort to think into and with (as well as against) Jaspers on a selected number of themes related to the central topic under investigation. In terms of such interpretative thinking there are, as James Collins notes, "several highways leading to the heart of Karl Jaspers' thought."[76] The path or outline of topics chosen here to elucidate Jaspers' thinking about religious pluralism is not found as such in any of Jaspers' works. It does not attempt to cover in detail all of the themes relevant to Jaspers' thought about religious truth, nor does it attempt to survey all of the texts relevant to the themes covered. Rather by focusing on a series of key topics, using selected texts, it attempts a series of probes, so to speak, each adding to a growing "feel" for the heart or nerve of Jaspers' approach to the question of pluralism and truth.[77] In the end, of course, the emphasis will shift from thinking into and with to thinking against Jaspers in the effort to evaluate his contribution. Yet that, too, is essential if one's own method is to remain faithful to the spirit and method of Jaspers' thinking.

The series of topics chosen as a path into the heart of Jaspers' thinking about religious pluralism and truth can be listed here, then, by way of conclusion to this introductory chapter and as an outline of the movement of thought through succeeding chapters. *Chapter II* details *Jaspers' own understanding of the problem* of pluralism and truth by examining his analysis of the crisis of our age and the new world horizon of convergence. Discussion focuses not only upon the problem as it emerges in this situation, but also upon what Jaspers regards as the new conditions governing thought about the problem which have become normative for this situation. In *Chapter III Jaspers' foundational thinking (Grundgedanke)* about and within those governing conditions is presented as the basis for all of his thinking about faith and truth. This foundation is itself a transcending thinking which culminates in the possibility of faith, the possible (existential) affirmation of transcendence, and thus the first clarification of the notion of existential truth. *Chapter IV* then examines in greater detail aspects of Jaspers' thought (on historicity, communication, and ciphers) which clarify the relevance of this understanding of existential truth to the *concrete particularity and plurality of religious truth.* Finally in *Chapter V* the *adequacy of Jaspers' understanding of truth* as a basis for the possible affirmation of a plurality of true religions is evaluated.

II

THE CRISIS OF OUR AGE AND THE PROBLEM OF RELIGIOUS PLURALISM AND TRUTH

> During the last few centuries...a single phenomenon that is intrinsically new in all respects has made its appearance: science with its consequences in technology. It has revolutionized the world inwardly and outwardly as no other event since the dawn of recorded history. It has brought with it unprecedented opportunities and hazards. The technological age, in which we have been living for a bare century and a half, has only achieved full dominion during the last few decades; this dominion is now being intensified to a degree whose limits cannot be foreseen. We are, as yet, only partially aware of the prodigious consequences. New foundations for the whole of existence have now been inescapably laid.[1]

The problem of religious pluralism and truth which was outlined in the preceding chapter must now be surveyed again, this time in terms of the details of Jaspers' particular way of conceiving the problem. To put the matter simply, if Jaspers' proposed resolution of the problem is to be understood and evaluated, there must first be clarity about what, specifically, he understands the problem to be. His analysis of the problem, moreover, is itself a not unimportant part of the contribution which he makes toward thought about the question of religious pluralism. The primary purpose of the present chapter, then, shall be to present and discuss Jaspers' understanding of the problem of pluralism and truth. Secondarily, of course, this presentation will serve as an introduction to some of the key themes which recur in Jaspers' thinking and to some critical questions which must be posed concerning that thinking.

After (1) some introductory reflections on the setting of Jaspers' analysis of the problem, the chapter will concentrate on (2) Jaspers' analysis of the crisis of our age and (3) the significance of that analysis for the problem of religious pluralism. The chapter will close with (4) some brief critical questions.

1.

The full scope and poignancy of Jaspers' conceptualization of the problem is to be found not so much in his "systematic" works as in his writings on history--those writings which in a variety of ways are an attempt to understand the unique and critical character of the present age in world-history.[2] For Jaspers sees the problem of pluralism and truth not as some isolated puzzle, but as one part of what can be called "the crisis of our age." It is only within this general crisis that the problem of religious pluralism arises in its modern form, and thus the full extent of Jaspers' understanding of the problem of religious truth can best be grasped within the framework of his analysis of the more general crisis. In fact, as one commentator has justly observed, Jaspers' sensitive attention to the radical novelty of the present age is "the vital soul, the explicit presupposition...upon which the great arch of his philosophy is constructed."[3] Thus it is not simply useful or helpful to begin a discussion of Jaspers' philosophy of religion in terms of his historical analysis of the present crisis; it is a necessary starting point. In the words of Hannah Arendt, one of Jaspers' most distinguished pupils, "it is against this background of political and spiritual realities of which Jaspers is more aware than probably any other philosopher of our time, that one *must* understand...the presuppositions of his philosophy."[4]

A brief clarification of this necessity may be useful, both to avoid misunderstanding and to provide a context for discussion of Jaspers' writings on the present age. The necessity of this starting point does not derive from the historicist cliché that a thinker can be understood only in the light of his times. Nor does it derive simply from the fact, true in itself, that an understanding of the historical situation which occasioned and shaped a man's thinking frequently provides a reliable path toward an adequate interpretation of that thinking. Rather, Jaspers' thought on the problem of religious truth must be seen in terms of his understanding of the present age because the former grows out of and is inseparably related to the latter. Put in general terms, for Jaspers what might be called the "philosophical" is inseparable from the "historical" or the "political." Since he first published his three volume

Philosophie simultaneously with *Die geistige Situation der Zeit*, his writings have always been concerned both with the technical matters and perennial questions of philosophy and with the social, cultural, and intellectual realities of the present age. As noted in the preceding chapter, his attempt has continually been to think perennial issues within the unique reality of the present.[5]

Failure to take cognizance of the shock of events and the deep challenges to thought which the real history of our era forces upon us is precisely what renders much merely academic philosophy existentially irrelevant--just so much scholarly trivia or lofty, but empty theory. In contrast to such philosophy, Jaspers sought to return to a more classical sense of theory which refuses the distinction of theory and politics, which sees the political as a matter "of central significance" for philosophical thinking.[6]

Such thinking always "starts with our situation"[7]--not only with general consideration of the situatedness of all thought, but with specific consideration of the realities of this concrete situation.

> We must remain aware of our epoch and our situation. A modern philosophy cannot develop without elucidating its roots in time and in a particular place.[8]

Yet such thinking is not "timely" or "existentially relevant" as a superficial reflection of the age, an identification of philosophy and history, of *Geist* and *Zeitgeist*. In terms of such faddish existentialism parading its relevance as significant thought, Jaspers' philosophy has always been "untimely--untimely from the start, untimely in principle" because its goal is "to bring to mind what has an ultimately timeless meaning."[9]

> Even though we are subject to the conditions of our epoch, it is not from these conditions that we draw our philosophy....We must not adjust our potentialities to the low level of our age, not subordinate ourselves to our epoch, but *attempt, by elucidating the age, to arrive at the point where we can live out of our primal source.*[10]

Thus Jaspers' position characteristically mediates between two extremes: the historicist identification of philosophy and history and the claim to timeless truth by those scholastic metaphysicians for whom history is essentially irrelevant.[11] Both the reality and limiting conditions of the present, which must be taken seriously if thought is to be significant and responsible, *and* the goal of thinking the eternally true within those limiting conditions are essential characteristics of philosophical thinking. In this sense the task of philosophy is always a hermeneutic one. It is the task of re-appropriating past traditions of thought in terms of present realities, yet always in an effort to attain the never finally graspable eternal source and goal of all history and thought.[12]

Such mediation is, Jaspers would argue, imperative today because of the critical character of the present situation. On the one hand, the very tumult and confusion of the present make it tempting for thought to seek secure refuge in recourse to timeless truths or the mechanical repetition of past verities. On the other hand, the radical break with the past ("the most profound caesura in history to date"[13]) which is at the root of such confusion makes it equally tempting to reject the past entirely in the name of a thinking more relevant (and true) to a totally new era in human history. For Jaspers, however, it is crucial that both temptations be resisted. The entire effort of his thought, and especially his extensive studies in the history of philosophy,[14] can be understood as a passionate effort to make possible a re-appropriation of the great heritage of human thought and belief within the radically new conditions of the present. He had nothing but scorn for those deluded romantics who believe that humanity can arise anew only when the rubble of the past had been swept away.[15] "The idea of progress" was, as Golo Mann notes, "foreign to him."[16] Yet the crisis of the present age *is* real and radical. The need to re-appropriate the past arises from the changed situation; the difficulty of the task from the radical character of that change. "The old world is lost for good; we must try to cling to memories across a chasm."[17] "It is impossible to return to a fancied past and to withdraw from the fundamental conditions of the age."[18] Serious thought cannot escape, but must come to grips with those new conditions.

2.

For Jaspers, then, the crisis of our age is the inescapable context for thought about religious truth. Yet this crisis itself is no simple, univocal thing which can be neatly described and clearly understood. In fact we cannot understand the crisis as a whole, with "scientific" clarity, because of its complexity, but even more because it is *our* crisis--both as a situation within which we stand (and not something we can contemplate from the outside or after its completion) and, even more significantly, as a crisis of our self-understanding (a loss of familiar sign-posts, an uncharted course).[19] We can and must, however, take our bearings in the light both of what can be known with cogent clarity and of what can be intimated from the deepest sources of our humanity.[20]

In some senses, of course, many periods of history can be regarded as critical turning points, periods of darkness in the dissolution of one culture and the struggle for the emergence of something new. There is, moreover, a perennial temptation to regard one's own time as *the* crucial point in history. For Jaspers, however, the present age does constitute a unique dividing line, a radical upheaval and a revolutionary turning point in human history as a whole--"the most profound caesura in human history to date." It is a period unparalleled in human memory, an "Age of Technology" which might be compared only with that hypothetical "Promethean Age" when the discovery of the tool set in motion the millennia-long process whereby the foundations of the great ancient civilizations and of (recorded) history were laid.[21] It is, moreover, the end of such history as the separate histories of different civilizations and the *de facto* beginning of global or world history in the "single unit of communications" constituted by modern technology.[22]

The present age is most evidently a "crisis" in the popular connotation of the word. It is a break, a separation, and thus an end and a loss. Jaspers describes the break as "monstrous" and as "disastrous" in its first effects.[23] "It is a period of catastrophic descent to poverty of spirit, of humanity, love and creative energy...as if the spirit itself has been sucked into the technological process."[24] Men have lost their bearings. The spread of industrial technology, the advent of the world-wide factory transforming all of society *and humanity itself*, has "deprived man of all roots. He is becoming a dweller on earth with no home."[25] "He still lives among stage props left from other times, but they have ceased to set the stage for his life."[26] The supposed liberation from old needs and received structures has proven less a liberation than a levelling, reduction, and loss. Jaspers summarizes this initial, destructive aspect of the present crisis by noting two interrelated facts: 1) the emergence of the masses from the destruction of communities and peoples, and 2) the dissolution of traditions in the "melting pot of nihilism."[27] Thus, ironically, there has been a terrible "loss of reality in an age of apparently heightened realism."[28]

Yet the crisis is a turning point--not simply a turning *from*, but also a turning *to*. What is to come is not clear. It cannot be clear since it is not something determined by the "forces of history" or the "cunning of reason," but a matter of freedom and destiny. It is clear, however, that humanity stands at a crossroads of terrible significance, and certain aspects of that crossroads are visible. It is above all a crossroads before which humanity *as a whole* stands. For with the universal spread of science and technology--the levelling of local and regional differences, the forced unification of the world through economic relations, communications, and the technology of total war--comes the emergence of a world situation for the first time in human history. Explicit and compelling convergence has replaced the isolation and merely relative or implicit unifications of previous history. It now conditions all thought and action. "Today, for the first time, there is a real unity of mankind which consists in the fact that nothing essential can happen anywhere that does not concern all."[29] The radical break with the past is not, then, just a "decline of the West." It is a world-wide phenomenon. The West, so to speak, not only united the world by exporting its technology, but simultaneously "exported to the four corners of the earth its process of disintegration."[30] Yet the crisis, which in the West developed gradually over centuries and from within the matrix of Western thought and belief, broke in the non-Western world with sudden fury as an attack from without at the deepest foundations of the fabric of life and thought. And this fact has only intensified the radically critical character of the present crossroads.[31] "The whole of mankind...all the old cultures have been drawn into this one common stream of destruction or renewal."[32] For that, in essence, is the crossroads--destruction or renewal; the loss of humanity itself as we know it in the reduction of existence to a totalitarian life-order (a "universal and homogeneous state") or the possible emergence of the substance of our humanity in new forms adequate to the new conditions of existence.[33]

Jaspers' understanding of this crossroads is nowhere more fully developed than in the context of the "schema of world history" which integrates his philosophy of history.[34] As he himself stresses, thoughts about the present age "acquire their full weight as elements of a total conception of history."[35] Such a "total conception" cannot, as already noted, attain the status of compelling knowledge. It is rather a sketch, based upon the most extensive factual knowledge, which seeks orientation in history toward the whole, the origin and goal, the unity and meaning of history, and thus elucidates the dangers and possibilities of the present.[36] Jaspers' schema is itself, then, a product or manifestation of the present crisis, both insofar as it represents an attempt to take bearings within the darkness and confusion of the age and insofar as it attempts to present a vision of history adequate not only for the West, but for all of mankind in the coming global era.[37]

The first and perhaps most significant task of the schema, then, is the determination of an axis of history which is truly universal--"a fact capable of being accepted as such by all men" and thus capable of providing a common basis for a common or convergent future.[38] The Christian axis which has dominated Western understanding of history is not adequate, for "the Christian faith is only one faith, not the faith of mankind."[39] Nor can the axis be founded on any other particular faith if it is to provide a common basis for the future communication of a plurality of faiths.[40] It is to be found, rather, in the empirical facts of history as such, "around 500 B.C., in the spiritual process which occurred between 800 and 200 B.C."[41] This "Axial Period" (*Achsenzeit*) and with it the idea of a unity to *world* history is clearly visible to us because we stand outside of the history which flows from it. We stand, in other words, within the second great turning point around which Jaspers' schema is built--the radical turning which is the crisis of our age and which we cannot know fully because we are still within it. For Jaspers, then, the schema of "the history of mankind visible to us" has two foci:

> The first led from the Promethean Age *via* the ancient civilizations to the Axial Period and its consequences. The second started with the scientific-technological, the new Promethean Age.[42]

All that is commonly referred to as "pre-history" and "history" (prior to "world history") is encompassed by that first focal point, leading to and flowing from the peak of the Axial Period. The long, shadowy development of pre-history (the hypothetical Promethean Age) and the early stages of recorded history--or the separate histories of the three great centers of culture in what we now call China, India, and Europe together with the Near Orient--led to the plateau of the great ancient civilizations. These in turn established the pre-conditions in economic, political, intellectual, and religious life for the Axial Period. In fact it is precisely in their breakdown, in the chaos of invasions and the long instability of transitions that there occurs, simultaneously yet separately within the three great cultural spheres, a brief moment, so to speak, of earth-shaking lucidity which transforms the spiritual consciousness of humanity.[43] It is a breakthrough which gives that consciousness a form and shape which has since been normative for all of human history, indeed for the very idea of humanity. And it is this spiritual normativeness which enables Jaspers to find the axis of history in the transitional period, from 800 to 200 B.C., between two great ages of empire.[44]

In more concrete terms, Jaspers describes the Axial Period as a concentration of "the most extraordinary events":

> Confucius and Lao-tse were living in China, all the schools of Chinese philosophy came into being...India produced the Upanishads and Buddha and, like China, ran the whole gamut of philosophical possibilities...in Iran Zarathustra taught... in Palestine the prophets made their appearance, from Elijah by way of Isaiah to Jeremiah to

> Deutero-Isaiah, Greece witnessed the appearance of Homer, of the philosophers--Parmenides, Heraclitus and Plato--of the tragedians.[45]

Yet aside from such reference to individuals and the events or writings which expressed their existence and thought, Jaspers' discussion of the common element, the *content* of the Axial Period--*what* it is that makes it an axis for history--is vague, more evocative than descriptive, and deliberately so. For "the breakthrough" was always local breakthrough*s* occurring separately and uniquely in each of the three great spheres of the human spirit. More than that, however, it was in each case something which, precisely as a "breakthrough" in awareness--as a "transcending" awareness of the origin and ground, and thereby of the limits of human existence--precluded universal and dogmatic expression. Thus even if today, on the other side of the chasm and faced with possible convergence, we sense hints and guesses of a common content, the expressible contents of the axial heritage nonetheless remain clearly distinct and often in opposition.[46]

For Jaspers, then, what emerges in the chaos and upheaval of transition is an awakening in which the mythic and hitherto unreflected substance of humanity is transformed by lucid consciousness of origin and ground.[47] It is a transformation expressed in the great world philosophies and religions which emerge at this time. Common to all is a wonder and openness and questioning which plunges to the source or (to shift the image) seeks transcending comprehension of the whole. Common to all is a purity of passion *and* reason wrestling with the fundamental human situation. And common to all (to use Jaspers' most characteristic term) is *faith*. Yet this awakening, transforming, transcending faith is not one but many. In itself inexpressible, it becomes the concrete faith*s* which give form and shape to subsequent (and separate) histories.[48]

The histories which flow from the Axial Period, histories conditioned by the consolidation of new empires and the spread of faiths, are histories of remarkable organic unities--the great traditions in their continual flux of stagnation and renewal. They have endured until the present as the great matrices of human life. Yet it is precisely their authority and thus their ability to sustain humanity which is today everywhere in decline. For during the course of Western history, from roots peculiar to the West, conditions were gradually established for the emergence of something critically new, for that crisis which constitutes the second turning point in Jaspers' schema of world history.[49]

The specific origins of the present crisis are manifold and finally, as with all real novelty, enigmatic. Jaspers traces its roots in Western religion, Greek rationality, and a restless dynamism which has characterized Western history (in contrast with the relative stability and unhistoric character of the East).[50] Its more proximate origins, however, are to be found in those events beginning in the late Middle Ages and continuing, as if in a series of waves, "a flood that has repeatedly risen and threatened to overwhelm us," until the nineteenth century when a definitive break within the continuity of Western history was effected.[51] A central thread in those events, that which is specifically new and effective in the break, is the rise of modern science and technology.[52] And with the spread of modern technology on the tides of missionary activity, colonial expansion, capitalist enterprise, and world war the break was no longer Western but world-wide.

Consciousness of epochal change, itself a fundamental element of that change, has likewise grown gradually throughout the modern era.[53] Seen initially as a return (whether to primitive Christianity or to classical antiquity) and then as triumphal "Progress," the change was first understood as a critical rupture, a definitive break, in the last century--and then by two solitary thinkers, Kierkegaard and Nietzsche, whose voices went largely unheard until the storm had already broken in the tragic fury of first one and then a second yet more terrible world war.[54] It was they who saw that with Hegel something had come to an end. The traditions which had held men for millennia--growing from Athens and Jerusalem and merging in Christendom--were passing, indeed past. Christendom is dead, said the one; God is dead, the other. They saw (foresaw) not a revolutionary leap forward, but a time of darkness, the loss of all footholds and bearings, the chaos of shrill voices and the stupefied drudgery of mass life--the endless round of production and consumption in the twin cults of performance and pleasure. Yet their importance rests not alone, not even primarily on their sense of crisis, their dramatic ability to shock us from the dogmatic slumber of thinking that the past can be continued with but slight adjustments. It rests, rather, on the depth of their understanding of the nature of the crisis. Perhaps better said, *their* sense of crisis was no mere external sense of alarm, but a profound understanding of what the present has become. They are radically different from each other, share no common doctrine, and indeed teach no systematic doctrine at all. Yet in two ways they go together to the heart of that turning which constitutes the inner movement of the present: 1) in their relentless *criticism* of the pretensions of reason (their sense of history's pervasive relativizing and of humanity's endlessly self-deluding construction of absolutes) and 2) in their ultimate recourse to individuality and *freedom* when all foundations and horizons have been criticized, relativized, "seen through."

An image utilizing the spatial contrast of "outside" and "inside" may serve here to clarify and crystallize Jaspers' understanding of this second great turning point in his schema of world history.[55] The crisis is a turning from past to future over the crossroad of the present. Seen from the outside this turning is the radical breakup of cultures, the end of an epoch of human history. It is the decline of authorities, hierarchies, structures, forms of life--the dissolution of those organic wholes, communities and traditions, which have formed and sustained political and social and religious life for more than two thousand years. The pivot, so to speak, upon which this turning moves is the emergence of science and technology as something radically new and compelling. Yet the crisis would be seriously misunderstood were it seen as something simply, or even primarily economic or political or social. Rather the development of modern science and technology and the subsequent rending of the once unified fabric of social life are fundamentally incomprehensible apart from radical changes in thought and belief. The crisis cannot be understood from the outside alone, as something external. It must be grasped from the inside, as a crisis of the human spirit, as "the great metamorphsis *of humanity* into which we are all being pressed."[56] This is not to suggest that changes in the realm of the spirit (the "ideological superstructures") are the most telling consequences of basic (technical, "substructural") changes. Rather the crisis itself is *fundamentally* one of the spirit.[57] Modern science and technology are not something external to man, but emerge from and are themselves part of a radical change in human consciousness.[58] The crisis, then, in its deepest sense is an "anthropocentric turn."[59] And the pivot upon which this ("inside") turning moves is the development, in various ways, of critical (historical, relativizing) consciousness.

Thus while the Axial Period was a profound transformation of human consciousness in the lucid emergence of faith, this second great turning point is also a profound transformation of consciousness. It is an emergence not of faith, but of critical consciousness--a shift in the foundations of consciousness as conditions of the possibility of faith. The substance of our humanity at stake in this turning is still faith (or its absence), but it is no longer present "out there," secured on metaphysical foundations and enshrined in dogmatic formulations. Rather, if faith is to be at all, it must be realized within new conditions, within that shift which is the inner core of the present crisis.

Of course the factors which have contributed to and make up this shift in human consciousness are many and Jaspers typically resists any neat formula or single theme.[60] It has already been noted that endless criticism and the recourse to freedom in the thought of Kierkegaard and Nietzsche "go to the heart of the present crisis," and the shift has been described as an "anthropocentric turn," an "emergence of critical (historical, relativizing) consciousness." Yet the meaning of these descriptive terms needs further elucidation.[61]

The development of modern science is, of course, always central to Jaspers' thinking about the present. For modern science arises within this shift in consciousness and by its pervasive presence forces, to so speak, recognition of and clarity about the shift. Said again: while the actual spread of scientific technology has "physically" disrupted traditional moorings, the reality of modern science as compelling, generally valid, and methodologically self-conscious knowledge--what

Jaspers refers to not as some hypostatized "Science" nor simply as so many definite sciences, but as the "universal scientific approach" (*Wissenschaftlichkeit*)[62]--has effected a critique of the possibilities of reason. It "transforms all traditional thinking" and "has changed the state of all truth ever handed down to us."[63] It results in a "universal methodological consciousness"--an awakening from naive or dogmatic slumber, a deep sense of the limits of all knowledge, and thus a rejection of traditional metaphysical and religious claims to the status of knowledge and universal truth.[64]

Yet the rise of science and the critique of reason *in themselves* are neither the whole nor the heart of that anthropocentric turn constitutive of the present crisis. They are, rather, inseparable from the long and complex development of the modern sense of freedom as individual autonomy. In Kantian terms, the first *Critique* leads necessarily to the second; knowledge is denied to make room for freedom. Not, of course, the empty freedom of mere arbitrariness, but that deeper freedom constitutive of the human self. For it is above all this sense of the self which epitomizes the shift in consciousness.[65] It is, initially at least, a freedom *from*--from natural necessity, natural law, and the constraining dogmatisms, authorities, and forms of traditional thought and life. Yet it is also, or potentially, a freedom *for*--for the possibility of historic self-realization and the endless quest for truth in those spaces or horizons opened by critical detachment and methodological clarity.[66]

It is, finally, the modern sense of history which recapitulates and concretizes the critically changed consciousness of reason and freedom. It is this sense, in part a result of the immense activity of the historical sciences and in part a consequence of the new global horizon established by modern technology, which relativizes and situates traditional beliefs and teachings in a manner well exemplified by Jaspers' own schema of world history and his writings on the present age.[67] Lessing's infamous "ditch" (*Graben*) runs down the center of that chasm separating us from the past. What were once objective realities and eternal verities have become relative and ever-changing creations of the human spirit. History, not nature, is the mobile home of humanity--the record of human striving and the field of human freedom.[68]

Thus the present crisis when seen within Jaspers' schema of world history is an almost total remaking of the external and internal conditions of human existence. Past unities have been destroyed; world unity of some kind is inevitable; and a new awareness of limits, a pervasive sense of relativity, and a fundamental conviction of autonomy govern life and thought. In itself this establishment of new conditions is not progress; neither is it decline. It is, rather, deeply ambiguous, the basis of that ambiguity which, as noted above, characterizes the entire present turning point in human history and leaves us at a momentous crossroads. Initially and tragically destructive, this turning has nonetheless clarified new possibilities. Criticism denies the possibility of metaphysics, reducing knowledge to the limited accuracy of objective and technical rationality (*Verstand*). But it also clarifies the possibility of a larger, transcending sense of reason (*Vernunft*). Freedom leads to isolation, alienation, the narrow confines of privacy and the emptiness of merely arbitrary commitments. But it also opens the possibility of that existential radicalization of freedom which (for Jaspers) is the sole road to transcendent truth. History severs the roots of tradition and casts one adrift in endless possibility. But it also makes possible the free reappropriation of those roots in the living struggle of communication with other traditions and truths. The present crisis opens a way through the terrible fires of nihilism to a purified possibility of transformed and renewed faith.[69] The "new age" may well be the graveyard of freedom and faith, an iron cage of total control and universal levelling--from the twilight of the West to a global night. Or the present darkness may presage a new, world-wide dawn.[70]

Jaspers devoted his life's work to the struggle for that dawn.[71] And there was for him (as already noted at the end of the first section of this chapter) only one general path in that struggle, a path leading to the future via the past. Pure rebellion against the darkness, however tempting and understandable, is no more adequate than paralyzed resignation.[72] Nor can the struggle be escaped by either a mechanical repetition of the past or a total rejection of the past in the name of progress or of some supposedly new departure.[73] "We must," rather, "try to cling to memories across a chasm."[74] We must rekindle the flame of the Axial Period "amid the utterly new conditions of (human) existence."[75] The task is extremely difficult because the break is real, the new conditions really new. Yet there is, for Jaspers, no other way in the present. It could even be said that the most general or fundamental of the new conditions determined by the crisis is precisely the necessity of this struggle to recover the past. This dialectical holding together of a real, definitive break and a necessary continuity is, for Jaspers, the cross of the present, the challenge of our fate.[76]

3.

Jaspers, as already noted, devoted considerable attention to religion in his later years as a direct result of his understanding of this challenge of the present age. His analysis of religious pluralism is part, a very important part, of that struggle to recover the past, and his understanding of religious truth is worked out within those new conditions which constitute our present. In a very real sense, then, all of the essential aspects of Jaspers' understanding of the problem of religious pluralism and truth have already been discussed. They need only be recapitulated briefly and made more explicit at several points.

The present crisis is quite evidently a crisis of concrete faiths and especially of those religious faiths which have illuminated humanity's three great spiritual spheres since the Axial Period. These great traditions have shattered under the impact of modernization.[77] It is a story often told: loss of religion among the masses, the secularization of daily life, the retreat of faith to the sphere of privacy as the window dressing of bourgeois culture. Yet, since "man is incapable of living without faith" of some sort,[78] the crisis is manifest not only in a decline of the traditional faiths, but also in their ossification and, more generally, in the decay of authentic faith into pseudo-faiths. Narrowly dogmatic and fundamentalist religion, the fanaticism of rigid political ideology, the distracting triviality of magic and superstition, or the desperation of chemical ecstasies and instant saviors--these are some of the forms of pseudo-faith (or unfaith) to which men retreat in a blind, almost reflex groping for fixed stability amidst the vertigo of loss and change.[79]

Such fixation has, of course, always been a danger, for religion is nothing if it is not positive and institutional, letter as well as spirit. Yet particularly with the advent of the modern era the great religions have undergone a sclerotic rigidification induced by defensive posturing and internal fragmentation.[80] Organic wholeness or "catholicity" has been reduced to the narrow confines of "catholicism" (*Katholizitat*) or "orthodoxy"--spiritless formalism which binds and blinds, and betrays that soaring of faith once realized in the positive confines of rite and creed.[81] Tragically, and ironically, this defensive fixation has transformed authentic religious faith into something typically modern--the rationalized, objectifying ethos which thrusts toward total order, total planning, and the total levelling of the local, particular, and personal.[82] Thus rigid orthodoxy in whatever form--whether in the remnants of the traditional faiths or in the new religions which have sprung up in the vacuum created by their decline--has become one among many pseudo-faiths, ideological curtains veiling the actual loss of real faith. Where it is not already evident in the direct loss of faith, the crisis of the religions is clearly manifest in the chaotic plethora of old and new dogmatisms, and in the widespread loss of ability to distinguish the once great faiths from their degenerate forms and trivial or terrible surrogates.

Yet this crisis, as noted above, involves not only destruction, but the possibility of renewal, the possibility that the great religious faiths might be transformed and thus reappropriated within those conditions constitutive of the present. "What the millenniums have disclosed to man of transcendence could once again become articulate after it had been assimilated in changed form."[83] In fact, as Jaspers notes, the very "brittleness" of the religions might facilitate the emergence of new forms from "the shells of their dogmas and institutions."[84] Such renewal is, moreover, not simply desirable as one aspect of the general struggle for faith in this time of darkness; it is crucial for that struggle. The religions have been the bearers of the axial heritage. They have shaped the continuity and handed on the substance of faith. Even where (in the West) faith has sprung up independently from religion, as philosophical faith, it has been made possible only by the institutional and cultural continuity of religion.[85] Philosophical faith depends upon religion for the "sociologically effective transmission of the contents indispensable to man which occurs solely through religious tradition," solely because these contents "live in the people through religious faith."[86] Thus today "what will become of the churches may decide the Western fate" and will certainly be crucial in the East where the distinction of philosophy and religion has not (yet) been realized.[87] "Hence the great concern about the vigor and veracity of ecclesiastic faith."[88] And it is this concern which makes the fact and problem of religious pluralism a matter of central importance for Jaspers.

Religion must be renewed *today*, within the conditions constitutive of the present. Yet those very conditions make a heightened and problematic awareness of religious pluralism inescapable. The new, global horizon has forced the great religions from their splendid isolation (and exclusivity), and the development of critical consciousness has forced a recognition of the rational and historical limits of all truth claims (and thus rendered universal and exclusive claims suspect). In a sense, the new situation created by the present crisis makes a realistic appraisal of pluralism not only necessary, but also, for the first time, a serious possibility. Said again, a real religious pluralism is a serious possibility for the first time in human history because of those conditions which have destroyed the relative and partial universality of the different traditions.[89] Such pluralism in the renewal and mutual communication of the great faiths is the goal, or one crucial goal of the struggle for faith in the present crisis. But this renewal can be achieved and this real pluralism attained only via the *transformation* of the great religious faiths, by the re-formation of their self-understanding in terms of those conditions governing contemporary life and thought.

> Since the transformation in our objective living conditions goes so deep, the transformation in our forms of religious belief must go correspondingly deeper in order to mold the new, to fructify and

> spiritualize it. A change is to be expected in what we have called the matter, the dress, the manifestation, the language of faith, a change as far reaching as all the other changes that have taken place in our era.[90]

> In the age of science and technology [the great religions] cannot stay as they are. Their coming change will be more profound than any past one, or else they will perish.[91]

The character of this transformation cannot be foreseen in all of its dimensions. It will occur, if at all, within the ongoing life of the religions, in the struggle of religious persons for the truth of their faith. Thus it is a matter about which the philosopher, as an outsider, can only speak hesitantly, aware of the inadequacy of what he says.[92] Yet one aspect of the required transformation is, for Jaspers, very clear (and he is not hesitant in asserting its necessity). It is given with those very critical developments which inescapably condition life and thought--given with the distinction between (universally valid) science and (absolutely, existentially valid) faith and with consciousness of historicity. It is the *necessity that the claim to exclusive and universal validity be renounced.* Not until "the poison of exclusive claims" is removed will the truth of religious faith be preserved and renewed for the present and future of humanity.[93] Yet with this renunciation and the transformation/renewal it makes possible, there arises, as noted, the possibility of real religious pluralism--the affirmation that more than one religion can be true.

Jaspers, of course, does not claim that this transformation will be easy. Not only has the present crisis caused the traditional faiths to become even more rigid and exclusive, but "the claim to exclusivity belongs in fact to the nature of authority" and to the relationship to transcendence by which authority justifies itself--and this is *a fortiori* true for religious authority.[94] Nor does his assertion of this necessary transformation demonstrate or at least clarify its possibility. On the contrary, it raises again the question about the meaning (logic) of the word "truth" when used with regard to such transformed religious faith. That question is taken up by Jaspers in his more systematic discussion of faith and truth, and particularly in his struggle against the (prevailing)

Christian understanding of revelation.[95] (It is that systematic thinking-through of what has been referred to here as "the conditions constitutive of our age" which is taken up in the next chapter.) It is clear, however, that for Jaspers the politically and historically crucial goal of such thinking within the present crisis is to "seek the ground on which men of every religious persuasion might meaningfully meet around the world, ready to recommit themselves to their own historic traditions, to purify them, to transform them, but not to abandon them."[96] "The situation of our times makes such a transformation--of biblical religion for us Westerners, of other religions for their believers, of philosophy for all--almost palpably evident."[97]

4.

There are various critical questions which might be raised regarding particular aspects of Jaspers' understanding of the problem of religious pluralism and truth, regarding the very idea of a crisis and the schematic conception of history.[98] At this point, however, it must suffice to raise in a preliminary way one question (or a series of related questions) which bears directly on Jaspers' approach to the question of religious pluralism. It should be clear, from remarks made above and in the preceding chapter, that Jaspers' understanding of the problem of religious pluralism within the broader horizon of the crisis of our age, his refusal to treat it as an academic or a narrowly religious question, is here taken as a significant contribution to thinking about religious pluralism. What must be questioned is neither the fact of the crisis nor its significance for thinking about religious pluralism, but the adequacy of Jaspers' interpretation of that significance.

The crux of Jaspers' interpretation of the present age is his joint affirmation of both a radical break and a necessary continuity with the past, of both fundamentally new conditions and the possibility of transforming and reappropriating past traditions within the new conditions. It is this dialectical holding together of new and old which, for Jaspers, makes possible an affirmation of both religious truth and religious pluralism. Yet it is precisely *this* holding together, *this* particular dialectical conjunction of old faiths and new conditions which must be questioned. Jaspers' intention, of course, is not the emergence of some synthesis in the form of a new, universal faith, but the possibility of particular (and plural) existential realizations of faith emerging in the conflict of traditional forms and new conditions. But the extent to which this intention can be realized within the framework of his thinking is open to question. Perhaps the old and the new are finally and fundamentally irreconcilable. Perhaps such dialectical thinking veils this irreconcilability and constitutes an evasion of the hard choices and real alternatives confronting us in the present crisis. Perhaps, while the strength and attractiveness of Jaspers' thinking derives, as he himself stresses, from the axial past, his effort to retain that past within the new conditions of the present may well blur the "decisive difference" between them.[99] Perhaps, finally, such "reappropriation" of the past would not be simply a dialectical negation of its form and transformation of its substance, but a negation of both form and substance, a loss of the truth *and the plurality* of the old faiths within the (normative and universal and exclusive) truth determined by the new conditions.[100]

This line of questioning can be pursued somewhat differently by asking whether, in fact, Jaspers' understanding of the present crisis is sufficiently deep or radical. On the one hand, then, it might be argued (as above) that his grasp of the crisis is not radical enough since he does not admit the fundamental irreconcilability between the new conditions and the traditional faiths. Thus, while he proclaims the significance of Kierkegaard and Nietzsche, he does not accept *their* assessment of such fundamental irreconcilability. Rather he neutralizes their real significance by categorizing them as "exceptions" and thus effectively dismisses them with lavish praise.[101] On the other hand, however, it might be argued that Jaspers' view of the present crisis is too deep, and this for two related reasons. In the first place, and despite his own repeated warnings against any total knowledge of the present, his understanding of the crisis absolutizes those "necessary and inescapable conditions constitutive of the present" in an almost monolithic historicist fashion. Thus, as suggested above, the very universality and necessity of these conditions would seem to negate any real plurality. The transformation required of all (particular and different) traditional faiths would effectively render them just so many forms of a general, existential faith.[102] Secondly, however, while Jaspers may indeed have understood the deepest and most pervasive currents constitutive of our present situation, they may not constitute a monolithic necessity for thought. It may well be not only possible, even if extremely difficult, but necessary to think outside of and in resistance to those currents (or conditions) if one is to adequately understand the logic of religious truth and the plurality of religious traditions.

At this point, however, these questions about Jaspers' framework for understanding the problem of religious pluralism and truth remain tentative and hypothetical. We do most evidently live in an age of crisis which has revolutionized the conditions of existence, shaken the great religious traditions, heightened awareness of religious pluralism, and cast doubt upon the very idea of religious truth. In this age, as Jaspers observes, a necessary transformation of the religions is "almost palpably evident." Yet the character of that transformation, the way in which truth and pluralism are best understood, is not "palpably evident." Jaspers' position on that transformation is clear enough. Yet the point of these questions is that his position is not without serious difficulties. The conditions or the modern consciousness within which he re-interprets religious truth may in fact be more part of the problem than part of the solution. Thus the way in which he understands the problem of pluralism and truth may exemplify that critical ambiguity in Jaspers[103] whereby one part of his thinking (his affirmation of "present conditions" and "modern consciousness") betrays the general intention of that thinking (to affirm religious truth and pluralism). What he wrote of Nicholas of Cusa may prove to be true of himself: "His insights lacked the power to penetrate the deceptions of his time."[104]

Jaspers, of course, recognizes the difficulties involved in these questions. The very real tension (and the irreconcilabilities which are real or final) between past and present indicate, he would say, the depth of the chasm separating us from the past and the very real dangers involved in the present. Yet there is, he would still argue, no other way to the recovery of faith than through the realities of the present. His life's work, as already noted, can be seen as an effort to understand and articulate those realities as a "common ground" or a "common framework so broadly based that historically heterogeneous faiths could communicate in it without abandoning themselves."[105] It would, in other words, provide a logic which reconciles plurality and truth. The *Grundgedanke* to which we now turn is one articulation of that framework.

III

THE PHILOSOPHICAL FOUNDATIONS OF FAITH AND TRUTH

While Jaspers' understanding of religious truth is naturally exemplified and clarified in his explicit discussions of religion, it is above all in certain recurring foundational ideas that the basis for that understanding is established. It is to those foundational ideas or, better said, that foundational thinking,[1] that attention must now be turned in an effort to map out the contours of the logic of religious truth.

The crisis of the present, as noted above, consists in the radical shaking of all previous foundations and the emergence of new conditions governing life and thought. It is that crisis, with its urgent struggle for the recovery of faith and the unprecedented possibility of a "common framework" for the communication of historically heterogeneous faiths, which has determined for Jaspers the present task of philosophical logic--"the discovery of a simple, essential, and comprehensive foundational thinking."[2] Said another way, while Jaspers' philosophy proposes no one system or set of doctrines, there is still a continually recurrent pattern of systematically thought and controlling ideas which are its determinative basis, "the ideas which govern its development."[3] It is, then, these ideas or patterns of thinking which establish the possibility of a plurality of true religions by distinguishing between the universality of truth in science and matters of fact and the absolute, yet never universalizable, character of truth in matters of faith.

The purpose of the present chapter, then, is to present those central ideas of Jaspers' foundational thinking which at once open the way to a possible affirmation of transcendent (and thus religious) truth and exemplify the logic of Jaspers' approach to that affirmation. Yet the methodological remark made in both preceding chapters bears special reiteration here. No attempt is made at a complete discussion of Jaspers' foundational ideas. What follows is not a review of the various paths of foundational thinking traced by Jaspers, nor is it simply a repetition of one of those. It is, rather, the effort to trace *a* path of foundational thinking, what Jaspers himself at one point calls "a typical sequence of fundamental philosophical questions,"[4] and thereby to recapitulate, in an exercise of systematic thinking drawn from various parts of Jaspers' work, the basic content, structure, and direction of that thinking. Thus the bulk of the chapter is devoted to (1) a presentation of a sketch of Jaspers' foundational thinking. This presentation is followed by (2) a brief discussion of the notion of existential truth which flows from such foundations and (3) a review of some critical questions which must be raised about them.

1.

Because the character of Jaspers' foundational thinking is not so straightforward or uncomplicated as the image of "foundations" might suggest, some preliminary remarks are appropriate by way of introduction. The term "*Grundgedanke*" comes to the fore in Jaspers' later writings--in the effort of *Von der Wahrheit* to articulate the foundations for a comprehensive philosophical logic and in subsequent works (including *Philosophical Faith and Revelation*) where he employs the categories first fully developed in *Von der Wahrheit*.[5] It refers specifically to that "basic philosophical knowledge" which is an "elucidation of the encompassing" in its various modes.[6] Yet Jaspers' foundational thinking can in no way be construed as something limited to or newly developed in that later work. All of his philosophical work is, as already noted, an attempt to think systematically to and from the most basic foundations of the human situation.[7] This, of course, is especially true of his two masterworks, *Philosophie* and *Von der Wahrheit*. And while the question of the relationship of these two works is a fascinating and important question for scholarship devoted to Jaspers' life and the development of his philosophy, what is significant for present purposes is their essential unity as expressions of that single movement of foundational thinking which achieved various forms for various purposes throughout his work.[8] Thus the idea of foundational thinking under consideration here is not limited to one work or one period of Jaspers' work.

It is the controlling set of ideas which pervade all of that work.

This point about the fundamental unity of Jaspers' various works can be made in another way which will further characterize the notion of foundational thinking. Although mention of "controlling, foundational ideas" might easily be taken to suggest some basic set of doctrines, Jaspers clearly does not intend that his *Grundgedanke* be understood in that way.

> All past ways of the basic knowledge were linked with a knowledge of Being. They were ontologies. Our modern basic knowledge can make no such claim; its character is different.[9]

As a movement of thought, foundational thinking clearly and necessarily involves contents or centrally recurring ideas and themes, and such ideas, thought systematically, are easily schematized after the manner of a basic set of doctrines. Yet for Jaspers, as already noted, although ideas, thought structures, and teachings are necessary, "the point of reference lies not in the doctrine itself, but in the possible goal of the motion."[10] The ideas or contents of thought are instruments for the accomplishment of that movement, like "a ladder which is to be given up after it is used."[11] The result is "not an expoundable doctrine but a movement of thought, a movement to be entered into...if one is to understand its meaning."[12] Such a movement of thought cannot be captured in any final set of doctrines, as something won and possessed. It can only be communicated indirectly, through various and differing systematizations of foundational thinking. Thus Jaspers' foundational ideas are conceived and employed in a manner which seems deliberately designed to frustrate the hunger for doctrine and to necessitate their being thought (in the active and suggestive sense of "thought through").[13]

In one sense, then, there is and can be no one *Grundgedanke* because that which such thinking intends--the basic, the ground, being--cannot be known. Even Jaspers' foundational thinking taken (as here) as a loosely unified whole must finally, he insists, be seen not as *the* sole foundation, but only as *a* foundational thinking. It remains in principle incomplete, in suspension (*Schwebend*).[14] Yet for Jaspers the essential unity of this thinking is found in its dialectical character as "intellectual operations which transcend the limits of the knowable...so that through these limits we become aware of the phenomenality of empirical existence and hence of the encompassing nature of being, thus entering into the area of faith."[15] This dialectical movement of transcending in thought beyond thought is, as Dufrenne and Ricoeur note, "the fundamental operation" of Jaspers' philosophy.[16] It is the central, unifying movement in that recurring pattern of ideas which constitutes a foundational thinking or a "basic philosophical knowledge."[17] Its goal is "not the cognition of an object, but rather an alteration of our consciousness of Being and of our inner attitude toward things."[18] It is a transformation of consciousness, a (self-) critical turnabout (*Umwendung*) which clarifies our basic human situation, the limits of knowledge, the possibility and nature of faith, and thus the possibility and nature of religious truth.[19]

A. Fundamental Situation, Basic Questions

Lest, however, such preliminary characterization of Jaspers' foundational thinking remain too abstract, it becomes necessary to turn to the actual contents of a typical pattern of such thinking which begins with a description of the basic situation of human existence. Jaspers is fond of quoting a story told in Bede's history which compares "men's present life on earth" with the picture of a medieval hall, a blazing fire warming within but dark night and a raging storm outside.

> Then a sparrow flies in and swiftly flits through the hall, in one door and out the other. For the moment of being indoors it is safe from the wintry blasts; but after the quick passage through the short, pleasant span it disappears from sight and returns from winter to winter. So too this human life is but like one single instant. We do not know what has gone before nor what will follow.[20]

Foundational thinking begins with this basic situation of the momentary, ever changing, fundamentally dark or problematic character of human existence. Or, perhaps better said, it begins with the fundamental experience of the inescapable situatedness of human existence.

> When I become aware of myself I see that I am in a world in which I take my bearings...I wonder and ask myself what really is. For all things pass away, and I was not at the beginning, nor am I at the end...though I can neither fully grasp my situation nor see through its origin, the sense of it oppresses me with a vague fear. I can see the situation only as a motion that keeps transforming me along with itself, a motion that carries me from a darkness in which I did not exist to a darkness in which I shall not exist.[21]

Jaspers' starting point clearly reflects the insecurity and anxiety of the present age, yet it is not intended simply as a reflection of contemporary experience. That experience, rather, is itself a reflection of the truly fundamental and thus perennial human situation--a situation too easily forgotten in the self-deceiving securities of less troubled ages.[22] Jaspers both echoes and calls upon the great traditions of religion and thought in describing this basic, as yet not analyzed, experience of the fragmentary, incomplete, "irresistably fluid" and thus threatening character of the human situation.[23] It is not an experience of unity, wholeness, or being, but of the "tornness of being" (*Zerissenheit des Seins*) in endlessly changing appearance.[24] "The fact is that we are everywhere confronted with fissures, cracks, which somehow penetrate the presumed integrity of being."[25]

Yet there is, so to speak, another, equally fundamental component in this basic situation described by Jaspers. Existence is problematic or questionable to human experience because that experience is always already founded in a question or a quest for that unity which overcomes fragmentation or that whole which grounds constant flux. The experience of existence as fundamentally problematic presupposes even as it awakens the possibility of such basic questioning. The experience and the questioning are the two inseparable and interdependent components of the basic situation. Neither is given automatically or necessarily. They do not arise as such in the daily "getting and spending" of empirical existence (*Dasein*), nor is their significance demonstrable to the "clear and distinct" calculations of consciousness-in-general (*Bewusstsein Überhaupt*). Yet the shock of events may plunge awareness to a deeper level, awakening that questioning which "changes man's inner condition."[26]

Such questioning can, of course, take many forms. Jaspers typically structures his writings at different times around different sets of basic questions. There are those "formulated by Kant with, I felt, moving simplicity: 1. What can I know? 2. What shall I do? 3. What may I hope? 4. What is man?"[27] Again there is the threefold exploration of the question of *being*, the question of *truth*, and the question of *reality*.[28] Or in most abbreviated form there is the single *Grundfrage*, "What is being?"[29] In whatever form, however, such basic questioning is not concerned with matters of fact, questioning about this or that. It arises, rather, at the limit of factual knowledge or worldly activity and is a limit or boundary questioning (*Grenzfrage*) about the whole or origin or ground of the realm of facts and activity. In the flux of time it is a question about that which transcends time. Within the multiplicity of truths (*Richtigkeit*) it seeks truth (*Wahrheit*); in the diversity of realities (*Realität*) it seeks reality (*Wirklichkeit*); amidst beings (*Seienden*) it seeks being (*Sein*).

Even more noteworthy, perhaps, is the fact that such basic questioning is not disinterested metaphysical speculation. "If it is true that the problem of the human situation is always a metaphysical question, it is equally true in reverse...that *the metaphysical problem of Being is an existential question*."[30] It is a deeply, passionately interested quest, arising more in dissatisfaction and anxiety than in wonder. It seeks not simply to know more, but to be more. It arises from the inner awakening of the fundamental passion of reason (as distinct from understanding or consciousness-in-general) and of Existenz or freedom.[31] It is inseparably the drive to know and the will to be--the deep and restless passion of the self "to think, to act, to live so that salvation" will be attained.[32]

Thus the basic situation which constitutes the point of departure for Jaspers' foundational thinking already involves an inner and transcending movement of thought. The starting point is not automatically apparent and cannot be demonstrated objectively. It rests, rather, upon that inner awakening and transforming of the self which is at once an awareness of the fragmentation and darkness of the human situation and a quest for that which overcomes fragmentation and darkness. The polarity of subject and object, of self and world, around which all of Jaspers' thinking is structured is already plainly in evidence, as is also that tension between situatedness in the world (in the polarity of subject and object) and quest somehow beyond the world which provides the dynamic for that thinking. It is already clear, too, that the real center of Jaspers' thought is that inner source or force which is constitutive of the (autonomous) human self. As Marcel observes, "for Jaspers it is only in the level of possible existence [Existenz] that a passion is engendered which causes the question of being in itself to issue into an act which transcends all objectivity."[33]

B. The Critical Turn

Yet if the anthropocentric turn constitutive of contemporary thought is already evident in the starting point of Jaspers' foundational thinking, it becomes, as critical turn, the explicit content of the first step taken from that point of departure. For while he calls upon the great traditions of religion and thought to evoke the basic situation, Jaspers moves immediately thereafter to those "new conditions constitutive of present life and thought" for further clarification of that situation. Thus while foundational thinking begins with the awakening of basic questions, it continues not in direct pursuit of an answer to those questions but by critical reflection on the questions themselves.[34] It was possible for traditional philosophy to be "both naive and truthful" in the direct pursuit of metaphysics, but those new conditions outlined in the previous chapter and referred to collectively as the rise of critical consciousness preclude such directness.[35] It is, in fact, only in the failure of such pre-critical pursuit of fundamental questions that critically conscious and truthful philosophy (and religion) can arise today.[36]

Such critical consciousness is manifest, of course, in various forms. It is present most generally in the diffuse climate of skepticism and doubt characteristic of the present crisis. It is present more specifically and more fundamentally in the rise of historical consciousness and the corresponding loss of the sense of world as nature, as purposeful whole (*cosmos* and *telos*) within which man might ultimately find bearings, albeit after great wrestling with the fundamental questions. Thus the world has come to seem not just provisionally fragmented, but fundamentally disenchanted. The endless diversity of indifferent objects into which man is thrown remains silent. It mediates no presence, holds no echo of a word which might speak an answer to the crucial questions arising from the human situation.[37] Such answers, rather, arise in abundance from the realm of human history. Yet the very plurality of the answers, or the heightened modern consciousness of that plurality, casts critical doubt on the possibility of any real answer and makes the basic questioning itself seem a futile exercise.

For Jaspers, this critical turn which brings the basic questions themselves into question receives it sharpest focus from the experience of modern science. Yet it is above all reflection on the character of that science which serves not simply to clarify the limits of knowledge, but actually to permit the recovery, with greater clarity than was previously possible, of those basic questions in which the transcending of thought and faith originates. The emergence of science, in other words, has forced a critical re-examination of the ways of knowing and seeking truth. The classical (Western) differentiation of philosophy and theology has been expanded to the "modern tripartition" of science, philosophy, and theology.[38] The result is not a negation of the possibility of philosophical and religious truth, but a critical clarification of the nature or logic of that truth vis-à-vis scientific truth.

Jaspers' full discussion of science is lengthy and complex, and has been itself the subject of detailed study.[39] Essential for present purposes is, first of all, the realization that scientific knowing has inescapably or irreversibly become the normative paradigm of knowledge as such. To know fully is finally to know scientifically. This is not, of course, to deny the knowledge given in the immediate experience and enjoyment of present and particular realities.[40] Yet the human drive to truth pushes beyond such immediacy in quest of cogent certainty and universal validity regarding the regularities and interconnections of things and events. It pushes, in other words, to rigorous inquiry by means of clearly defined methods in the gathering and assessing of evidence. Thus "the aim of scientific inquiry...is to bring the objective evidence to a clear condition; where it imposes itself upon the impartial mind with compelling force."[41] It is, in fact, the note of cogency (and thus of universal, *because* cogent, validity) which Jaspers stresses as the most central characteristic of scientific knowledge.[42] Yet he takes great pains to debunk the caricature of absolute cogency purveyed by the popular misconception of science as some monolithic (almost magical) system of absolutely certain truths. Cogency remains an ideal which guides scientific endeavor, but is in fact always relative and limited.[43] It is the very ideal of cogency which requires clarity and definiteness, attention to the differences in realms of knowing, and recourse to particular methods appropriate to particular realms of objects. And it is these characteristics of the actual sciences which stand in marked contrast to the myths of scientism.[44] There is no one Science. There are, rather, the various sciences in each of which the goal of cogency is achieved, or at best approached, by the methodological limitation of inquiry to particular, relative fields or perspectives or realms of objects. The significance of modern science is "the idea of compelling, generally valid cognition proceeding by specific methods, progressing infinitely, but always particularly...."[45]

If, then, scientific knowing is the normative paradigm for all knowledge because of its compelling, universal validity, it attains that character precisely because it is always and in principle limited. It is limited by always specific and diverse horizons of theory and method and by the consequent endlessness of possible inquiry which makes any unity or universal system of knowledge impossible.[46] More fundamentally, it is limited because "only that which is definite can become an object of our knowing."[47] Only that which appears or comes to focus in the forms and categories of thought can be known. In Jaspers' preferred Kantian terminology, only the phenomenal is knowable.[48] Thus while research makes "a presupposition of the knowability of the world," this presupposition is only correctly understood to mean "the knowability of objects in the world" and not "the knowability of the world as a whole."[49] The "world as a whole" is not only never attained in the endlessness of determinate inquiry, it cannot even be thought without contradictions. It is, rather, as Kant showed, a limit-concept or a regulative idea which serves to guide or lure the thrust of knowledge toward unity, but can never itself become an object of knowledge.[50] The world that can be known is the phenomenal realm of endlessly diverse objects. "All our knowing remains *in* the world and never attains *the* world...for our knowing the world is fragmented (*Zerissen*)."[51]

Thus clarity about the nature and significance of science--what Jaspers calls the "universal scientific approach" or the "scientific attitude" (*Wissenschaftlichkeit*) as distinct from the sciences themselves, and what is here more generally referred to as "critical consciousness"--leads to clarification of the basic human situation and of those fundamental questions emerging in that situation. Initially that clarification seems entirely negative. The basic questions are not only unanswered, they seem unanswerable. Any claim to *know* answers to such questions about the human situation *as a whole* can today result only from self-deception. It is no longer possible to be both "naive and truthful." Critical clarification of the nature of knowledge shows such basic questions to be limit questions, not simply in the sense that they arise at the limits of specific, this-worldly knowing and doing, but in the more fundamental sense that they point beyond the boundaries of knowledge as such. As far as we can *know* they are empty, indicating nothing but our limitation to the objective realities of this world--"our imprisonment in appearance."[52] They would seem as futile as the quest for the invisible gardener in Flew's interpretation of that infamous parable[53]--unanswerable in principle and thus logically meaningless despite the seeming significance with which they arise in the basic situation. In the darkness of that situation, then, the light kindled by the spark of the basic questions would be extinguished by the cold breath of criticism.

Yet unlike Flew, Jaspers' thinking does not terminate with this first critique of the basic questions. In fact, as noted above, it might be said to begin in earnest only with the initial failure of these questions. For with Kant, the denial of knowledge is a preliminary clarification which makes room for faith--or, more accurately, for the possibility of freedom within which faith might arise. It destroys the misunderstanding whereby the basic questions are thought of as continuous with the quest for knowledge. Yet this disillusionment makes possible a shift or transformation of consciousness, an inner awakening whereby the basic questions may now be authentically appropriated as a quest for truth (*Wahrheit*) other than the correct and cogent truth (*Richtigkeit*) of knowledge.[54]

There is, of course, no proof, no universally compelling argument or evidence at this juncture in the critical turn of Jaspers' *Grundgedanke*. Thrown back upon oneself in the fragmented darkness of the world, without the security of clear and objective answers to one's fundamental questions, it may not be possible to make the pseudo-enlightened claim of positivism that the human situation as a whole is exhausted by the empirically knowable. It is possible, however, to remain (with Flew) in an agnostic stance. Indeed such a stance has the seeming honesty, even nobility, of a clear-headed acceptance of limitation to the human world of knowing and doing, and of refusal to lose oneself in "endless theological controversy" or "metaphysical and mystical nonsense." For Jaspers, however, it is precisely the refusal made by such "passive agnosticism" which constitutes a loss of oneself in the real endlessness of "knowing and doing."[55] Thus, for instance, scientific knowing is, when taken by itself, an absurd endlessness in the dual sense of a ceaseless *and* purposeless accumulation of a more detailed and diverse knowledge. Refusal to take seriously the fundamental questions which arise in the face of such endlessness is not only a denial of that basic will to unity and truth which is constitutive of science,[56] but as such it is a denial of the self of the scientist, or of that human depth in the self whence arise both that basic will to truth and the consequent basic questions about the human situation.

Equally possible at this juncture, of course, is the existential exaltation of freedom or will in face of the world's endlessness and the seeming unanswerability of the basic questions. Jaspers' rejection of such existentialism has already been noted. Purporting to rescue the self, the defiant claim to absolute autonomy leads in fact only to despair. It fragments the deepest self, turning freedom against reason, the will to self against the will to truth. Denying the claim of those basic questions wherein the self awakens to itself, it severs the root of human seriousness. "Absolute independence drives me to despair. I am aware that as flatly self-based I would have to sink into the void."[57]

Jaspers himself has been accused of such irrationalism championed in the face of the absolute limits of knowledge.[58] He would claim, however, that the critical clarification of knowledge leads not to the negation of reason, but to the opening of possibilities for reason deeper than those of knowledge. The basic situation is not changed. Rather the inner awakening given in that situation is radicalized. The basic questions can now be understood as existential questions not simply in the evident sense that they are questions of deeply personal concern, but in the more radical sense that they can only be answered by that depth of the self which Jaspers calls "Existenz." Said another way, the failure of knowledge and clarity about its immutable limits open the possibility of a different type of question and answer, a questing and finding which is not a matter of knowledge, though it is preeminently a matter of reason and truth, and also of freedom.[59] Thrown back upon oneself, without the security of objective knowledge, one is faced anew, yet with a clarity which makes it seem as though for the first time, with the basic questions. One is faced with the possibility of and need for decision--not about this or that, but about the ultimate significance of one's entire existence and the significance of reality as a whole. In such an awakening there is, Jaspers insists, the possibility of a non-cognitive, therefore non-cogent and not universalizable, but nonetheless true answer to the basic questions.[60] There is, in other words, the possibility of faith. It is, then, the elucidation of that possibility opened and clarified by the critical turn which constitutes the next step in Jaspers' foundational thinking.

Before taking that next step, however, it will be well to pause briefly since it is now possible to clarify somewhat further the way in which this foundational thinking was previously characterized. The possibility of truth opened in critical reflection upon the fundamental questions is not something which can be demonstrated or shown. It is, rather, a possibility which can be realized (brought to awareness as it is achieved) only in deed, in an inner action or movement of self-realization which is an act of freedom because of the absence of compelling knowledge. Neither that which is intended in this action (the whole, or ground sought in the basic questions), nor the source of the act (freedom or Existenz) can be known.[61] Thus its possibility, while opened in critical reflection and made an object for thought (but not for cognition)[62] in the various patterns of thinking which seek to elucidate, evoke, suggest, and even provoke it, is finally given only in the free, personal act in which it is realized. As act, moreover, it is never possessed finally in the way in which knowledge might be said to be attained. It is, rather, always only historic realization, ever again to be realized or reenacted.[63]

It becomes clearer, then, why Jaspers insists that his foundational thinking is not a matter of ascertainable doctrine, but a movement of thinking. Its communicable thoughts would elucidate or suggest what cannot be known, only realized, and that realization itself is an act, a moment in a movement of thought or, better yet, the action of the movement itself. Foundational thinking, in other words, both as the communicable thoughts and the inner action indicated and suggested in those thoughts, is *transcending*, not in the ordinary sense that any thought intends an object which transcends the thinking subject, but in the more specific and fundamental sense that it "means to go beyond objectiveness."[64] Yet thought cannot move "beyond" objects of thought, except to that which becomes another object of thought. Thus the movement of thought "beyond" itself must return to, or better always remain within thought, within the thinking of objects. It succeeds only insofar as it constantly "circles," or moves as an endlessly dialectical negation of itself which "stands on the boundary," "floating" or "in suspension" (*schwebend*) between objectivity and the non-objectifiable.[65] It succeeds, moreover, not simply as the movement of such thinking, which by itself would be vacuous. "It will be true only if it is translated into concrete transcending," only if it is accompanied by the "second wing" which is personal Existenz.[66] (And conversely the "second wing" would be blind without such thinking as the presence of the first.)

The *Grundgedanke* is already such transcending, although perhaps not self-consciously, in the first awakening of basic questions, and the dialectic of transcending continues through the critical turn to the self-conscious awakening of Existenz and the final affirmation of what Jaspers calls "transcendence." "There is only one transcending," but that single action may be said to have "three modes [which] not only follow one another, but each subsequent one gives new meaning to the one before."[67] Thus there is first of all the critical transcending of objectivity in clarification of the limits of knowledge and awareness that the basic questions seek answers which are not possible objects of knowledge. Even in this first mode, however, the point of transcending "is not so much to test the inadequacy of objective representations as to transform oneself....It is an act upon oneself which makes a man another man...."[68] This inner transformation becomes focal in the second mode of transcending, the elucidation of Existenz as the full awakening of the possibility of quest and answer which are no longer matters of knowledge. In its turn, then, that awakening already contains the completion of transcending in its third mode, in affirmation of that transcendence which is the ground of both objectivity and Existenz. It is these latter two and inseparable modes of transcending which are opened by the critical turn, and their elucidation in thought is the subject of the next step in foundational thinking (just as their realization in act, in possible Existenz, is the object or goal of that thinking).

C. Existenz and Transcendence

If the *Grundgedanke* is not empty speculation but thinking as a real part of one's own life, then Existenz (the "second wing") is already present in that thinking as the source of basic questions and of the drive to the limits of knowledge, just as transcendence is already present as the anticipated goal of those questions and that drive. Yet Existenz is most fully, or self-consciously present (the self comes most fully or deeply to itself) in what Jaspers calls limit or boundary situations (*Grenzsituationen*). Put somewhat differently, the self which experiences *definitive* boundaries is not the practical self of everyday activity nor the knowing self of object consciousness. It is Existenz. And as Existenz in boundary situations it stands, so to speak, always already before or in relation to transcendence. "Thus to exist [Existenz] and to find oneself before transcendence are one and the same, just as to experience boundary situations and to exist are the same."[69] In Jaspers' discussion of boundary situations, then, the completion of this typical pattern of his foundational thinking can be found.[70]

For any human being, of course, to exist means to be in ever changing situations, to interact with one's situation, to move from one situation to another. Yet this general situatedness of existence is not the same as a boundary situation.

> [Boundary situations] *never change*, except in appearance. *There is no way to survey them* in existence, no way to see anything behind them. They are like a wall we run into, a wall on which we founder.[71]

While we can change, even overcome particular situations by knowing and doing, boundary situations cannot be thus known, acted upon, and overcome. They are experienced as boundaries only by Existenz which is awakened in them. They are fully experienced, in other words, not by analysis which shows them to be inescapable limits "for all human beings," but by a leap or shift to a uniquely personal realization that they are *my* boundaries, in which I realize the final powerlessness of *my* thoughts and actions, and perceive the fundamental precariousness of existence as *my* fate.[72]

The first and most fundamental of such boundary situations is the inescapability of situatedness as such--not as some abstract principle but as the realization of *my* concrete, historical, situatedness, *my* determination in this particular situation, here not there, now not then, as man or woman, with these parents, this heritage, this religion (or no religion), this language and culture. I act within these situations to know and change them. Yet it is precisely in such action that I experience my situatedness as a boundary, as inescapable, personal historicity. I remain ever determined and particular even as I transcend that determination at least in knowing that it is a boundary, "a wall *we run into*." I can, of course, reject this awareness and lose myself in getting and spending, knowing and doing. Or I can awaken to the strange mystery of myself, ever limited (imprisoned) in the narrow confines of my particularity, and thus face "the choice in which I accept or reject my definite existence as my own," in which I curse or love my fate.[73]

Within this fundamental boundary situation are other, particular boundary situations, each throwing me back upon the strange reality of my uniquely individual self and throwing that self into question. Thus the silent irreversibility of *death* is a boundary when actually experienced in the death of one I love or above all in the possibility of my death. So, too, *suffering* as my lot and constant companion becomes a boundary in its inevitability. And in action I experience both the absolute necessity of *struggle* and the unavoidability of *guilt*.[74] Nowhere in the world do I experience security or rest or harmony which is whole and unbroken.

> In every boundary situation, I have the ground pulled out from under my feet, so to speak. There is no solidly extant existence I might grasp as being. There is no perfection in the world...the boundary situations everywhere show existence to be inherently dubious and brittle....[75]

The "dubiousness and historicity" of all existence, then, is the final, most general boundary situation revealed in all previous boundaries. Jaspers refers to it as the "antinomic structure of existence" where all completion is always partial and relative, always countered by antithesis or negation: life by death, peace by struggle, joy by hopeless misery.[76]

Boundary situations, then, are a recapitulation of the basic situation wherein foundational thinking originated. It is the same fragmentation, darkness, and endless flux, but now experienced more clearly as an absolute boundary ("like a wall we run into") and, the same thing said differently, experienced as *my* boundary ("a wall on which we founder"). I experience my world, my existence, the only reality which is reality for me, as ever precarious, and finally unreliable. I experience the "constant threat" or "menace" which drives me "to seek security" and, finding none, to face "this absolute failure, which if I am honest I cannot fail to recognize."[77]

Each of the major boundary situations described by Jaspers is different, not simply reducible to an instance of a general type (in spite of their abbreviated presentation here). And each is actually experienced as a boundary only by individuals, in the uniqueness of their lives. Moreover, as already noted, the actual experience is for Jaspers finally ineffable, not something which can be known objectively.[78] Attempts to describe what happens at the boundary will inevitably be faltering and different, drawing upon ideas, categories, and comparisons from the realm of objective thought and from the diverse languages peculiar to each particular historic situation. Thus Jaspers' own discussion is itself, and self-consciously, only one such attempt to point toward the reality of transcending in boundary situations. The experience leads, he says, if one does not flee from it, to an absolute parting of the ways. "When boundary situations are experienced as such, there are two possibilities: the way to nothing and the way to authentic being."[79] I am led to a brink on which I founder, an abyss over which I am suspended, and am faced there with the basic questions which were never more totally *my* questions, questions about the total significance of my life and of the endless reality in which that life finds itself. I am faced, in other words, with a radical decision: defiance or acceptance? absurdity or significance? nothing or being?

At the juncture of this final decision, and it clearly need be neither in fact nor description quite so dramatic as both brevity and Jaspers' hortatory style make it seem,[80] two things are said to happen (or one thing with two inseparable aspects is realized). Existenz comes fully to itself, yet only by or in relation to transcendence. I realize myself in an unsurpassable manner as original, not defined by or in the world (although realized only in the world), as unique destiny. I realize myself in freedom, because this depth of individuality is manifest finally in the moment of decision without necessity or support. Yet I realize myself precisely as restless depth ever seeking its transcendence (or else I would not come to myself at the boundary). And I come to assurance about self-being in awareness that I am not my own ground, but that I and all of reality are indeed grounded. In coming to myself on the path of freedom I come to awareness "that I do not have myself alone to thank for my freedom either."[81] Rather "Existenz can grasp itself in its own freedom, only if at the same time, and in the same act, it will perceive something other than itself."[82]

Jaspers' formulations at this absolutely central point are startlingly simple and straightforward. No proof is possible; no argument is attempted. The truth as he sees it is stated clearly, almost dogmatically. In coming to self at the moment of absolute decision one affirms oneself as grounded, as having received oneself, as self related to transcendence, and thus one simultaneously affirms the reality of transcendence as transcendence (as always other, as that which is but not as what it is). Cases which would seem to contradict this affirmation are understood as being, in fact, covert instances of it. The suicide ultimately affirms the radically other by his total and absolute rejection of present reality.[83] So, too, affirmations of "the way of nothing" are dialectical assertions of the complete otherness of being.[84] And the attempt to ground freedom in itself destroys freedom.

> The test of the possibility of my Existenz is the knowledge that it rests upon transcendence. I close the door to my becoming Existenz if I take it for being proper....I cannot take freedom for the ultimate....Confined to itself, even freedom withers....Existenz is either in relation to transcendence or not at all.[85]

Again, no proof is possible. The assertion itself is but an invitation to enter into the movement of this transcending thinking, an invitation to experience an answer to the basic quetions in the ever momentary affirmation given at the culmination of that movement, at the boundary.

D. Faith

Foundational thinking, then, culminates in an affirmation of transcendence. Better said, it culminates in the "fulfilled absolute consciousness" of Existenz as assurance of self in relation to transcendence.[86] Such consciousness is, in some of

Jasper's many suggestive indications, love, absolute trust, fundamental assurance, awareness, and ascertainment. It is, in the designation which is most central for Jaspers' thought, *faith* as "love's explicit, conscious certainty of being."[87] Foundational thinking, then, culminates in faith.[88]

Such faith, as the platitude will have it, stands in contrast to knowledge. Yet the contrast is misunderstood if taken to mean that faith is *beyond* knowledge as its completion or *before* knowledge as its postulate or presupposition. Faith receives no vision of the supersensory which completes knowledge.[89] Neither is faith some (*a priori*) necessary and universal condition of the possibility of knowledge or consciousness.[90] Yet faith does come after knowledge in the sense that experience of the limits of knowledge awakens the possibility of faith. And it is prior to all objectification and mediation in the sense that it is original. It arises from an origin within and not as a consequence of something else (whether reasons or will).[91]

Nor should the contrast of knowledge and faith be understood as an antithesis, as if faith constituted an irrational alternative to or denial of knowledge. On the contrary both knowledge and faith arise in the one will to truth which is reason, and reason is indispensable to faith as it is inseparable from Existenz.[92] Reason is goad and guide in the transcending motion of faith. It forbids resignation and forgetfulness of basic questions, presses to the limits of knowledge, rejects preliminary or pseudo-answers, and drives to the depth and unity of truth which is transcendence. The passion of self-being which is Existenz would lose itself in blind self-assertion or fanatical ideology without the continued presence of reason as its polar complement. Faith as the consciousness of realized Existenz is thus impossible without reason.[93]

Faith and knowledge are contrasted, then, because they are finally incommensurate. Where knowledge is attained as necessity and retained as possession, the shift at the limits of knowledge to the possibility of faith opens a realm, so to speak, of freedom and historicity. Faith is attained in an inner, free act of transcending. It is not retained at all, but is an always momentary breakthrough as the consciousness of (ever-again-to-be-enacted) Existenz wherein the transcendent other through which man exists is disclosed. Thus it is an answer to the basic quest, but an answer given only in the continuing search "where this depth has opened and the search as such has become a finding."[94] While Jaspers will even at times speak of this answer as a "revelation,"[95] and more generally as a gift or something received, it is a revelation of transcendence, of an answer which always remains other, beyond our grasp. Transcendence, *as transcendence*, can only be actually affirmed in continuing search, in the movement of transcending awareness which is faith. In the very failure of the search to find an answer "the search as such has become a finding" of that which truly transcends. (Any other answer would constitute in fact a negation of transcendence.)

Since, moreover, boundaries are absolute and transcendence that which really transcends, man remains always *within* boundaries--*in* the world. "It is *in existence* only that I come to be sure of myself, and thus of transcendence."[96] The language of transcending does not mean transcending to another realm or another self (the ghost within the machine), for any assertion of such another realm would contradict the very idea of transcendence. It would constitute an objectification of that which cannot be objectified. There is, rather, only this world--existence--and insofar as Existenz and transcendence are affirmed, they are affirmed in the transformation of this world, as depth or "vanishing presence" which comes to appearance in the critical relativizing or suspending of knowledge and object consciousness. And faith, too, as consciousness of this transformation (or as the reality of transformed consciousness) is realized only in existence. It awakens only in thought and action and comes to expression only in the categories of thought and action. In other words, what is realized at the boundary as *faith* comes to expression (returning, so to speak, from the boundary) in categories of thought and action as *belief*. While it is in principle true that subsequent to the negative movement of transcending, and yet "prior to all objectification, possible Existenz has a sense of transcendence,"[97] it is also true that the movement of thought cannot be arrested at a theoretical still point. It must find positive expression in the world, in forms of objectification--above all in the great historic forms of religion and thought, by way of vision in art, poetry, story and song, and by way of speculation in the constructions of philosophy and theology.[98] The inescapable objectifications of faith are clearly not knowledge. They cannot be identified with that which they express.[99] Yet they are the indispensable medium of transcending faith--in which it moves, from which it springs, and to which it returns (to spring again). Thus faith, as culmination of Jaspers' foundational thinking, recapitulates the dialectical tension characteristic of the entire movement of that thinking. It remains "rooted in the vehicle of phenomenality" and thus, paradoxically, is an "always mediated, forever new immediacy."[100]

Such, then, in relatively brief overview, is a typical pattern of Jaspers' foundational thinking. The logic, or the basic structure and movement of that thinking has already been highlighted. Still, for reasons of both completeness and fidelity to Jaspers' text, it would not be well to leave this typical pattern without reference to the ideas with which Jaspers himself in his philosophical logic summarizes and schematizes that structure.[101] The following brief presentation of those ideas, then, which makes no pretense of adequacy, might perhaps serve to provide a concluding image for the central movement and direction of Jaspers' foundational thinking.

Jaspers begins with "an ancient philosophical insight, definitively clarified by Kant," that reality for us is phenomenal--that it is real insofar as it becomes an object for us, and thus that the subject-object dichotomy (or split) is a finally unsurpassable basis of consciousness.[102] (It is the basic human situation understood in terms of consciousness.) All is real for us only as it appears in consciousness, or, what is the same, enters into the dichotomy of subject and object. "What does not enter into this dichotomy is for us like non-being."[103] Yet by the same token, whatever becomes an object for us is appearance and not, to use Kant's phrase, *das Ding an sich*. In Jaspers' own terms, awareness of the subject-object dichotomy means simultaneously awareness of the phenomenality of all things ("imprisonment in phenomenality"), awareness that whatever appears can only be a particular form or appearance of being, something determinate, never that which really encompasses (or grounds) both subject and object. What is, as being itself, cannot be an object (for a subject) any more than it could be a subject (as consciousness of an object). Rather, "authentic being that is neither object nor subject, but that is manifested in the whole of the subject-object dichotomy" Jaspers calls "the encompassing" (*das Umgreifende*).[104] It is "that which, split into subject and object, becomes appearance."[105] It is, in a metaphor Jaspers employs only slightly less frequently than the figure of something encompassing, the source or origin (*Ursprung*) whence the split of subject and object arises.[106]

Of course awareness of the subject-object dichotomy and thus of phenomenality and the encompassing--real awareness as distinct from an idle repetition of formulae--is already the result of "intellectual operations which transcend the limits of the knowable...."[107] And such operations, whatever their specific content or context, all involve a turnabout in thinking (*Umwendung*) which Jaspers calls "the basic philosophical operation" (*philosophische Grundoperation*).[108] Thus any thinking which arises as basic questions in search of ultimate truth or reality or being will necessarily involve this basic operation "which is to ascertain the encompassing by transcending the object within the object thinking that remains forever inevitable...."[109]

> From the subject-object split, in which we aim at objects and are tied to them, this operation accomplishes the turnabout into the encompassing that is neither object nor subject, but contains both.[110]

To think the encompassing, of course, means to bring "it" within the subject-object dichotomy and thus to negate it as encompassing. Yet awareness of this contradiction compels one immediately to negate the result (the objectified thought of an encompassing reality) by repeating the basic operation of thinking beyond the subject and object. Thus the basic philosophical operation achieves no results. It is, rather, a constantly to be repeated dialectical process whereby "the realm of the objective must remain in motion, must evaporate as it were, so that as the object vanishes a fulfilled consciousness of being is made clear by this very vanishing."[111] It is, in other words, the central motion or act of transcending thinking.

Still, if awareness of the encompassing *as encompassing* is realized only in the critical operation or movement of thinking which turns back upon itself, even that self-critical awareness must take objective form ("the ambiguity of the objectified non-objectiveness"[112]) by being thought of "either as though it could become an object, or...as though it were the subject, visualized as an object. We have no other alternative."[113] Thus in his attempt to think the encompassing Jaspers elucidates various modes whereby we, in the dichotomy of subject and object, are encompassed--various basic experiences or basic, irreducibly original ways in which we are, so to speak, present in the dichotomy of subject and object and thus, correlatively, in which the encompassing is present as ground or source.[114] Such elucidation is not a deduction of modes from some one, essentially understood encompassing, nor does it make any claim to completeness.[115] It is, rather, an attempt to clarify basic experiences of being encompassed, and becomes compelling only in such clarification.[116]

Jaspers' discussion of the various modes of the encompassing is in itself a major and quite lengthy exercise in transcending thinking.[117] Its details are at times perplexing and at times fascinating as he outlines first the various "immanent modes" of encompassing, whether conceived subjectively as empirical existence (*Dasein*), consciousness-at-large (*Bewusstsein überhaupt*), and mind (*Geist*), or objectively as world, and then the "transcendent modes," again conceived both subjectively and objectively as Existenz and transcendence ("the encompassing of all encompassing"). Yet however much such detail might be necessary for a complete understanding of Jaspers' philosophical logic, it is not as such essential for the topic of religious truth. What is essential, and what has hopefully been reiterated in somewhat different and summary fashion by this brief mention of "the basic philosophical operation," is the basic movement *within* boundaries *beyond* them in which ultimate truth is affirmed in faith.

2.

Most of what needs to be said at this point about Jaspers' understanding of religious truth has already been dealt with either explicitly or implicitly in the preceding discussion of his *Grundgedanke*. Thus a brief resume will serve to highlight the characteristics of that understanding of truth most directly related to the question of religious pluralism.

The central point at issue, of course, is Jaspers' assertion that as a result of or, better yet, in the process of such foundational thinking "the very meaning of truth undergoes a change."[118] Truth can no longer be limited to the truth of knowledge. Rather "truth that is vitally important to us begins precisely where the cogency of cognitive consciousness ends."[119] Such non-cognitive truth is commonly called "existential truth," but Jaspers often prefers to speak variously of "absolute truth," the "truth of Existenz," "transcendent truth," or most simply "truth" (*Wahrheit*) in its fullest sense which is "infinitely more than scientific correctness (*Richtigkeit*)."[120] And for Jaspers it is the possibility of such truth which today opens the way for an authentic reappropriation of traditional faiths and for the affirmation of a possible plurality of true faiths as a context where those faiths might meet and communicate.

When Jaspers asserts that in foundational thinking "the very meaning of truth undergoes a change," he does not mean simply to say that in addition to cognitive truth there is now another type of truth, the truth of Existenz. His view is more complicated and interesting than that. In fact he describes a different sense of truth for each of the four subjectively conceived modes of encompassing.[121] Thus while truth is cogent correctness for the encompassing of consciousness-at-large, it is pragmatic or vital utility for empirical existence, conviction and the relative wholeness of ideas for *Geist*, and the unconditionality or absoluteness of faith for Existenz.[122] (And only in the mode of consciousness-at-large is universality a criterion of truth!)

Yet these different types of truth, although finally irreducible one to another because of the irreducibility for us of the various modes of the encompassing, do not simply stand unrelated side by side. Rather they overlap and interrelate in various ways, each being comparable to others at different points and all, finally, "in conflict: in possible reciprocal assaults upon one another."[123] Such conflict originates in the basic will to truth which is a will to the unity of truth, to the idea of the one truth, or the oneness of truth, which is given with our most fundamental sense of truth. This ideal of the one truth involves the tendency to conflict whereby each mode of truth seeks to establish its primacy by exclusion of the others. (Witness the pseudo-scientific scientism of our day.) Yet it simultaneously provides another instance of the by now familiar dynamic of Jaspers' thought. In this instance the irreducible plurality of types of truth (and not just a plurality of claims within the same type of truth, as in a plurality of religious truths) constitutes an absolute boundary which becomes a spring-board for movement to the unity of truth in transcendence. Given the persistence of plurality, the quest for (and assertion of) unity is paradoxical. It is the basic paradox which governs all of Jaspers' thought about truth: in time "we do not and will not have the one truth--yet the truth can only be one."[124]

Among the various types of truth, however, the truth of knowledge or truth in the encompassing of consciousness-at-large has a certain primacy at least insofar as all types of truth must come to thought and expression in the medium of such consciousness (as, too, thought about truth occurs only within this medium). Thus it is, as the *Grundgedanke* plainly shows, above all by means of contrast with cognitive truth that Jaspers clarifies the possibility of that truth of faith which is throughout his primary concern. When all is said and done, it is still this contrast which is crucial for Jaspers' thought.[125]

> Truth is either universally valid and identical for everyone--this is the type of scientific truth, which is always relative, however, true only for certain objects and under certain conditions, established by and related to certain methods. Or it is an absolute truth, by which the believer lives and realizes himself, but at the price that its statements, as rationally communicable tenets of faith, are not universally valid for all men. Absolute truth is historic, in other words, because we as possible Existenz are historic.[126]

Such absolute truth is, as already noted, not simply different from the truth of knowledge, but is made possible precisely by the latter's impossibility or limitation. "It is the absence of objective knowledge which is the condition of our freedom."[127] In the absence of constraints, freedom is possible. In the absence of supports and guarantees, in the constant dialectical motion where thought is suspended, so to speak, on the hyphen between "both" and "and" (or "neither" and "nor"), freedom may act absolutely or unconditionally. And in the absence of objective mediations, such unconditional action constitutes not only self-realization but mediation of transcendence. It is the inner spark struck amidst external darkness by whose dim light ultimate truth is affirmed.

Absolute truth, then, contrasts with the truth of knowledge not only because of the incompatibility of knowledge and freedom, but because such freedom is the point of contact with transcendence which is equally incompatible with knowledge. Absolute truth, in other words, is transcendent truth: the truth of transcendence attained in the motion of human transcending precisely as that which ever transcends human grasp.[128] Thus it is always historic in the sense that it is realized in action, in a moment in the motion of transcending, and in the correlative sense that it is realized in forms which themselves (objectively) remain historically relative vehicles, never identifiable with the transcendence attained in them.[129]

Here again, then, is the basic paradox governing Jaspers' thought about truth, this time in a form directly relevant to the discussion of religious pluralism. The truth of transcendence can only be one, yet transcendent truth is realized historically and thus its very realization prohibits universalization of the form of that realization. In different words, the transcending awareness of faith affirms absolutely the truth of the absolute (transcendence). Such affirmation must, moreover, take on specific historical form since Existenz remains always in existence. And while this necessity governs all faith, it is most clearly true for religious faith which, as already noted, is distinguished from philosophical faith by its eminently *positive* character.[130] Thus precisely because it is affirmed as the truth of the absolute (transcendence), its historic form cannot be proclaimed as exclusively (universally) true. On the other hand, because that which is affirmed is and can be affirmed absolutely only in some particular form, that form and only that form can be affirmed as true.

Strictly speaking, then, Jaspers does not assert a plurality of absolute, transcendent truths. Such an assertion would contradict the logic of existential affirmation. Yet as that logic precludes the claim to universality for what one affirms absolutely, it must allow the possibility of other such affirmations. Thus Jaspers can and does assert the *possibility* of a plurality of such truths. When speaking loosely, he at times adopts a language which has today become quite common--speaking of different faiths as so many paths to God or of "the deity which does not show the same features to all men."[131] Such statements, however, remain a shorthand for his more carefully nuanced position, and cannot be taken to mean that the philosopher (or anyone else) in observing the variety of faiths "from the outside," so to speak, is somehow able to know that many are true (because he knows the one truth they all share or manifest or symbolize). Plurality and absolute truth are not contradictory, yet the logic which allows that assertion prohibits the actual assertion of a plurality of true faiths. The actual assertion of transcendent truth remains an ever historic act of individual Existenz.

As regards religious truth and plurality, then, Jaspers' conclusion is obvious. Religion and philosophy, as the two fundamental paths of faith, are not reducible to some common form, some unifying foundational truth, any more than different religions in their diversity are reducible to some general, shared religious faith. Yet both are subject to the same fundamental conditions clarified by Jaspers' foundational thinking. In terms of those conditions it is no longer possible to be "both naive and truthful." Thus religious statements can no longer claim the status of knowledge, of something universally true. They can be true, rather, as forms and expressions of absolute truth, as uniquely historic and irreplaceable realizations of existential faith. Where religious truth has not previously been understood in such terms, its self-understanding must be transformed if it is to remain truthful.[132] In terms of such a transformed understanding of religious truth, however, a possible plurality of true religions can be straightforwardly asserted as the resolution to the problem of pluralism and truth.

3.

Yet this conclusion, while it follows directly from Jaspers' foundational thinking and would indeed seem to resolve the dilemma posed by contemporary consciousness of religious pluralism, is not without serious difficulties--difficulties, moreover, which finally extend to the most basic elements of that foundational thinking. For Jaspers' discussion of the logic of faith, precisely because it attempts to deal systematically with the deeper currents of contemporary thought, takes one to the center of today's most fundamental and controversial issues.[133] While fuller consideration of these difficulties must for the moment be deferred, some brief indications will serve to sharpen the point of questions raised rather tentatively in the preceding chapter and thus to focus the issue which must be taken up in the next chapter in order to flesh out the sketch of Jaspers' approach to the question of religious pluralism and truth which has been presented thus far.

The possibility of a basic contradiction in Jaspers' thought between intention and performance was already raised at the end of the last chapter. His intention as regards religious truth is clearly to provide a framework for the recovery of faith which would establish the possibility of a plurality of true faiths as one condition of that recovery. Such a framework is provided in the performance of foundational thinking which, by clarifying the fundamental conditions of truth which have emerged in the present age, clarifies the logic of the truth of faith in terms of which religious truth is to be understood and the possibility of plurality established. Yet it can be argued that the basic idea of absolute (or existential) truth clarified by this foundational thinking, far from establishing the intended possibility of a plurality of true religions, actually constitutes an effective negation of both plurality and religion. The logic of such truth, in other words, requires a transformation of traditional religious faiths by which they are in fact subsumed into the (normative and universal and exclusive) truth of Jaspers' philosophical faith.

Jaspers, of course, would vigorously reject this charge. Religion for him is and remains clearly distinct from philosophy. However much philosophical faith might be "religious" in the very broadest sense of that term, actual, positive religion "remains for philosophy always a polar other."[134] Thus philosophical faith can never become some "enlightened" natural religion ("within the limits of reason alone") designed as an alternative to the superstitions of positive religion. Moreover the truth of faith, whether philosophical or religious, is always attained within the boundary of particular historical situatedness and expressed in forms peculiar to each historical situation. Such truth, then, is inescapably "historic and plural."[135]

Yet even where these claims are provisionally granted, the basic problem has not been met. Granted, in other words, that philosophical faith provides no alternative to the rich particularity of religious faith and that all faith is attained only in historic particularity (and thus diversity), such particular philosophical and religious faiths are still true *only* insofar as they are instances or expressions of that more fundamental or foundational idea of truth outlined in Jaspers' *Grundgedanke*.[136] And that foundational truth, it can be further argued, bears little resemblance to and is actually inimical to the particular character of *religious* truth. Thus Jaspers' call for the transformation of traditional religious faiths would indeed, his disclaimer and his intentions notwithstanding, constitute an effective negation of both plurality and religion.

The central issue here concerns the significance of historic particularity (whether as particular expression of thought and belief, as concrete action and ritual, or as particular persons and events) in Jaspers' understanding of religious truth. (In different terms it is the issue of mediation and immediacy.) Without particularity there would be no plurality, and without certain types of relations to specific particularities there would be no religion.[137] Thus a logic which would affirm a possible plurality of true religions must provide an account of particularity which admits of a real or significant *plurality* which is also a *religious* plurality. Yet Jaspers' *Grundgedanke* seems vulnerable at just this point. His account of particularity seems open to serious question in (at least) two related ways.

In the first place, the endlessly dialectical character of his thought is intended quite explicitly to bring all particularity, all objective securities and solid footholds, into suspension. The continual movement is crucial since it alone finally brings one to the boundary, so to speak, to the point where the absence of securities opens the possibility of Existenz, and thus the possibility of an ascertainment of transcendence in faith. The concrete historical particularity within which one is inescapably situated, for instance, is possibly revelatory of transcendence precisely when it is recognized as a boundary situation--that is, precisely in the movement which seeks to transcend its particularity. Yet this would mean that transcendent truth is not at all attained *in* particular historical existence. At best the particular situation becomes an occasion or a necessary means--a springboard whence Existenz leaps to transcendence and to which it must always return, but only to leap ever again. To be sure, transcending for Jaspers does not, cannot mean actually moving beyond particularity. No direct, intuitive or mystical encounter with transcendence seems possible to Jaspers. Thus the springboard image is perhaps deceptive. Transcending is a movement *in* thought beyond thought which thus never really leaves the particular form of thought. It is, more broadly, a movement *in* the world which changes one's consciousness of the world, rendering it transparent to its depth (or encompassing). Thus there is never actually a moment when the particularity is behind. Nor, then, can the expression of faith in the forms of that particularity be regarded simply as an inescapable but clearly secondary consequence of some previous and in itself inexpressible experience of transcendence. Yet the particularity of the situation, the actual historic character which differentiates it from other situations, would still seem to be dissolved into a general structure of existential anthropology. What is important, indeed inescapable, is particularity as such, almost any particularity, and not this specific (and sacred) particularity. Thus particularity is still important only as a means in the movement of transcending, however much that movement remains "imprisoned in appearance."

Secondly, then,(and this is really the same point made somewhat differently) Jaspers' account of particularity would be inadequate because, however necessary or inescapable the given particularity, truth resides essentially in the movement of Existenz within that particularity.[138] The truth of faith is essentially a matter of inwardness or immediacy for which any mediations are simply necessary and finally indifferent occasions. Or, to put the matter somewhat differently, the sole "mediator" is Existenz. The inner movement of Existenz is the sole point of contact with transcendence. All other mediations are true only insofar as they occasion, serve as vehicles for, or express this single mediator, and they must be relativized or brought into suspension by the critical movement of thought lest they hinder the free emergence of Existenz as that single mediator. Thus while a plurality of mediators, of various particulars as necessary means in the movement of transcending, is certainly possible, it cannot be regarded as a significant plurality. All faiths have to meet the test of this one faith.[139] Thus, too, it is at very least seriously questionable whether such inwardness, reducing as it does particular religious mediations to the status of indifferent means, can constitute an adequate account of religious truth. The *sola fide* ("sola Existenz") of Jaspers' radical protestantism would seem to void the significance of *any* religious mediations.[140]

There are, then, serious difficulties involved in Jaspers' understanding of the logic of religious truth which make his claim to have established the possibility of a plurality of true religions questionable. Jaspers, of course, is not unaware of the type of objections which have just been raised and there are aspects of his thought which speak directly to them. Thus explicit consideration must next be given to those aspects if an adequate picture of Jaspers' approach to the question of religious pluralism is to be obtained.

IV

PARTICULARITY, PLURALITY, AND RELIGIOUS TRUTH

With the type of questioning indicated at the end of the preceding chapter the central issue in Jaspers' discussion of religious pluralism has been clearly joined. And while the main lines of Jaspers' response to such questioning were laid down in his foundational thinking, it is the elaboration of those foundations with regard to different, specific topics which provides the details of that response. Typically, of course, there are a variety of such topics wherein Jaspers elaborates the detail necessary for an adequate understanding of his thought on the central issue of particularity and plurality. For present purposes, however, it is above all the topic of *history*, and more specifically Jaspers' understanding of the *historicity of truth*, which will best serve to illustrate in detail his argument concerning particularity.[1] In what follows, then, aspects of Jaspers' discussion of history will be used to fill out the needed detail of Jaspers' affirmation of the possibility of a plurality of true religions. Reference will also be made to two related themes which figure heavily in Jaspers' thought and which bear directly on the question of particularity: his stress on *communication* and his idea of *cipher*.

Since Jaspers' various discussions of particular topics invariably follow or recapitulate, each in its own way, the basic, dialectical movement of his foundational thinking, the outline of this chapter will be structured accordingly. Thus Jaspers' response to the criticism that he loses particularity (and with it plurality and religion) will begin with (1) a brief restatement of his critical protest against all particular claims to the status of universal, trans-historical truth. Within that negation, however, he (2) affirms the possibility of necessarily historic and always particular (thus plural) attainments of absolute truth. (And the dialectical character of this affirmation is summarized in his understanding of all such historical events and beliefs as ciphers of transcendence.) Finally, he urges (3) the applicability of this understanding of truth and particularity to the specific case of religious particularity and truth, thereby reaffirming the possibility of a plurality of true religions.

1.

In essence, Jaspers' response to the charge that his thinking loses particularity[2] is given in the principle fundamental to his *Grundgedanke* that Existenz can be realized only in the world. "It is *in existence* only that I come to be sure of myself and thus of transcendence."[3] The distinction between Existenz and existence, in other words, indicates not a separation but a dialectical relationship. "Possible Existenz thus *sets itself off* from the world in order to find the right way into the world...as the medium of its realization...."[4] Paradoxically, then, "the world can be transcended only in the world"[5]--only in thought and action concretely engaged in always particular situations in the world.

This means, of course, that for Jaspers there is no truth to an image of transcending as a flight *from* the world, as some direct intuitive grasp of transcendence. In this regard his suspicion of and continual struggle against mysticism have already been noted.[6] Yet it is equally true for Jaspers that no final (a-historic) truth, whether in the form of particular events claimed to be revelatory of the whole or of particular ideas and beliefs supposed to comprehend the whole, is attainable as such *in* the world. The impossibility of such "metaphysical" truth is, of course, basic to his foundational thinking and is given with the Kantian critique central to that thinking. More concretely, however, that impossibility is a fundamental aspect of the modern historical consciousness which for Jaspers is one of the basic conditions for truth clarified by the contemporary crisis.[7] The world in which Existenz comes "to be sure of itself and thus of transcendence" is the world of human history. And all attainment of truth in that world can only be historic, never total or final.

The term "modern historical consciousness" refers, of course, to a phenomenon as complex in origin as it is in substance. And while Jaspers has written a good deal about the idea of history,[8] he typically has avoided any "neat" attempt to tie down the rather slippery concept.[9] It is at least clear, however, that modern awareness of history has contributed in a variety of ways to the widely accepted sense that all particular ideas, beliefs, and traditions (all religions, for instance) are in some sense historically relative. What was thought to be the eternal-in-time, those sacred points where the distance between time and eternity had been considered bridged, has come to be seen as itself temporal, changing, and relative to particular periods and places. Humanity lives not simply in time, but in history, that realm of human striving whose record is dotted with diversity. Each person, then, finds himself situated concretely at a particular time and place, with a particular heritage of language, culture, and beliefs, all of which are caught up in an endless whirl of change. Knowledge brings awareness of this situation, and awareness that it is just one particular situation lost, so to speak, in the vastness of history. Yet such knowledge can provide no way beyond this situatedness and thus threatens to produce a dizzying vertigo of relativity which leaves one naked and rootless.[10]

The danger of such historical consciousness, then, is that it can lead to a complete or totally inescapable relativism. Sometimes called "historicism," such total relativity clearly constitutes a nihilist denial of the very possibility of truth.[11] Yet Jaspers'own effort, as noted above,[12] is to steer a middle course between such historicism and an a-historical attainment of eternal verities. His thought is an attempt to take cognizance of the relativizing of traditional worlds, the tremendous growth of historical knowledge, and the consequent heightened awareness of the historically situated and changing character of human thought--to take cognizance of what is inescapable for historical consciousness even while overcoming the temptation to a complete historical relativism. Thus while wary of the constant threat of nihilism, he nonetheless clearly affirms the relativizing consequences of historical consciousness as a premise which must today condition the quest for truth.

Such consequences do not, of course, result simply from the vast accumulation of historical knowledge during the past several centuries. For historical knowledge as such, no matter how extensive, does not necessarily lead to historical consciousness (as the term is being used here). But neither can it overcome such consciousness. Thus it is not the fact of massive knowledge of history, but the critique of (or understanding of) the nature and limits of historical knowledge which is the logically necessary foundation for the modern consciousness of historic relativity. What can be known via historical investigation is endless factual objectivity about this or that--evidence of human action and of the multiple and complex interrelations of causes and effects. But that which transcends such endless relativity, either as the final whole of history or as the trans-historical which may speak at or through particular moments of history, cannot be thus known. In terms of religion, for instance, historical study can attain considerable knowledge (or truth) *about* a given religion or religious reality, but cannot know or even approach the truth *of* the religion itself (the religious truth).

> Confessions of faith are themselves realities and belong to history. But, whatever it is to which they bear testimony is no object of historical investigation.[13]

For knowledge, then, or as knowable reality, history is "the relativization of everything objective."[14] It is "ultimately nothing but...universal transience, change in causal relations of effect and aftereffect, an endless up and down in random diversity without beginning or end."[15]

Yet if the massive accumulation of historical knowledge is not the logically necessary foundation of modern historical consciousness, it remains nonetheless true that this increase in knowledge, coupled with the global horizon of awareness established by modern technique, has made this consciousness a dominant, crucial aspect of the contemporary crisis, no longer just the concern of solitary forerunners like Kierkegaard and Nietzsche. And the resulting situation has, in fact, led to the type of actual communication, as in the serious and respectful encounter between world religions, which if anything heightens not just a general sense of relativity, but specific awareness of the relativity and situatedness of one's own particularity.[16]

Vastly increased historical knowledge, then, as one key aspect of the pervasive consciousness of historic relativity, involves (at least) two serious risks.[17] On the one hand it may in fact lead to greater and greater distance from the past of one's own (or any other) tradition. It may constitute a "vast rubble to which events keep adding immensely, and which is no longer meaningful to know or collect."[18] At best a "collection of curios,"[19] it might block access to serious reappropriation of the past even as it filled the present with protean, but empty possibilities.[20] It might, in other words, lead to rootless indifference and absurd freedom.

Or it might, on the other hand, lead to a reaction whereby "what is historically known will be one-sidedly objectified and solidified into something valid and authoritative," into "a universal, generally human truth which I believe I know as a historically objective *authority*."[21] And while the temptation to such flight from history may well be perennial, it seems especially prevalent in the face of contemporary consciousness of change, diversity, and relativity. Such forgetfulness of history can, of course, take many different forms. The defensive rigidity of religious orthodoxy and the parallel emergence of fanatical surrogate religions, both in reaction to the uncertainties of the contemporary crisis, have already been noted.[22] Threatened by relativity, the proponents of tradition absolutize the contents of one tradition (and of one particular configuration of that tradition) into a universal validity, thus demanding a mechanical repetition of the past.[23] More generally, one quite legitimately takes the content of a particular historical moment, wherein truth may indeed have spoken and may continue to speak, but then illegitimately locks the vast diversity of human history into that one particular by identifying it as a literal embodiment of transcendence.[24] Or, moving in the opposite direction, one develops a philosophy of history which neatly harmonizes all relativity into the known unity of a vision of the whole. Thus all particular situations, including one's own, become instances of a general law or moments in the general process of history.[25]

Whatever its specific form, however, the essence of such response to historical consciousness is an illegitimate absolutization of what can in fact be known only as a relative, historic particularity. It is the response of procrustean absolutism in the face of protean relativism. And while Jaspers' entire philosophical effort can, as noted, justly be taken as a struggle against the nihilist consequences of the latter, his most vehement polemics are reserved for the former. Whether it is the dogmatic exclusivity of orthodox Marxism, orthodox psychoanalysis,[26] or orthodox Christianity, all such illegitimate universalizations of particular beliefs are excoriated as forms of that totalitarian tendency which Jaspers calls "catholicism" (*Katholizität*)--the forced unification of all diversity under the visible authority of one truth proclaimed as both absolute and universal.[27] In its effort to save (its) particularity from the abyss of relativism, it becomes forgetful of history and thus, ironically, loses the real historic particularity it purports to defend.

Jaspers, then, would turn the tables on his critics (since it is above all Marxists and Christians of various shades who attack him for the loss of concrete historic particularity). As understood by orthodoxy, the embodiments of particular traditions become fixed and rigid. They "congeal into general validities" which conceal rather than reveal the original inspiration and authority which spoke in them.[28] By absolutizing a particular vision of the whole, rigid philosophies of history reduce all actual particulars to *mere* instances of a general process. They lock the concrete and complex particularity of history into the procrustean pattern of certain particular events or some ideological straightjacket. Even more fundamentally, however, by the claim to know *the* truth and the consequent demand for assent and obedience, all such catholicism destroys that existential freedom and unconditionality without which, for Jaspers, not only particularity but truth as such would be unattainable.[29] By denying the concrete and relative particularity of one's situation, one ends "unexistentially tied" or "affixed" to "a universal truth existing in timeless unreality."[30] The result is "an unreal fantasy that would exclude any real Existenz...a fundamental, albeit unwitting, *voidance* of historicity."[31]

Thus Jaspers' defense of particularity begins with a reiteration of his basic critique of knowledge, this time in the form of a negation of the possibility that any historic particularity might claim the status of trans-historic truth.[32] The first line of that defense, in other words, is a critique of his critics and of the traditional defense of historic particularity. In view of the reality of history it is no longer possible to be both naive and truthful, no longer possible to defend particularity by proclaiming *the* truth of a given particularity. Rather it is the very relativity of all knowable history, the objective relativity of history, which Jaspers understands not as the demise of the possibility of truth (although the danger of collapse into nihilism is always present), but as the condition of that possibility.[33] Modern historical consciousness, clarified and made inescapable by the crisis of the present, has become the context within which the idea of truth must be reunderstood and the truth itself must be sought.

2.

Jaspers' argument to this point, however, has done little to meet the real force of the objections to which he is responding. The context of discussion, the shift in focus to the realm of history, is admittedly more concrete, but the problem of Jaspers' ability to provide an adequate account of particularity remains, and is perhaps even exacerbated by his stress on the relativity of all historic particulars. The concrete movement of history has replaced the inner movement of thought as the focus of Jaspers' dialectic (although the two are hardly separable), but continual movement, the loss of all fixed points and objective or historic securities, is still central as the fundamental condition which opens the possibility of a free transcending. Thus historic particularities, such as particular religious traditions, would still seem at best concrete occasions for such transcending. Given their relativity it is hard to see how they could be anything else.[34]

Yet for Jaspers, however abstract the description of transcending may inevitably be in foundational thinking, it is precisely the reality of such transcending in concrete history which refutes these objections. Thus the second, positive move in his response, and the real core of his account of the place of particularity in absolute (religious) truth, is his attempt to establish a *via media* between relativism and catholicism by a dialectical holding together of the absoluteness of faith with the objective relativity of history. It is a path to the attainment of truth not by somehow getting around the limitations of history, but by moving *through* history, by penetrating to the depth of the particular.[35] Jaspers elucidates the possibility of such transcending-in-penetration by means of his idea of historicity or existential historicity (*Geschichtlichkeit*) and the correlative notion of adoption or appropriation (*Aneignung*).

For Jaspers talk of the "historicity" of truth refers not to the relativity of history, but to the absoluteness of truth attainable within that relativity. "Absolute truth is historic, in other words, because we as possible Existenz are historic."[36] But that is to say that *for Existenz* historic truth can be absolute. Here Jaspers makes a distinction which has since achieved common currency in much contemporary (particularly theological) thought--the distinction between a "sense of history" (*historische Bewusstsein*) as knowledge of history and the historical truth of that knowledge, and a "sense of historicity" (*geschichtliches Bewusstsein*) as existential consciousness of one's historically situated particularity and the possible (historic or absolute) truth of that particularity.[37] That sense of historicity which is a condition and characteristic of absolute truth is not, as stressed above, a result of historical knowledge, however much the tremendous increase in such knowledge may have contributed to the clarification of such existential historicity. Yet a sense of history as both awareness of the plurality, relativity, and endless movement of history and a critical understanding of the limits of historical knowledge does set the stage for existential historicity and the attainment of historic truth. On the basis of such a sense of history an individual may awaken to awareness of his own historic situatedness--"as phenomenally bound in time to a sequence of singular situations."[38] He may, in other words, experience the fundamental boundary of situatedness in historic particularity.

Jaspers' foundational thinking has, of course, already shown how experience of this boundary can be the springboard to transcending in Existenz. Yet it can be this springboard only insofar as the concrete situation *in its unique particularity* becomes *in adoption* the medium of transcending. There is, then, a shift in the image which captures (or controls) Jaspers' thinking--from the spring or leap which leaves one in suspension on the boundary to penetration wherein one identifies with one's historic particularity, from solitary inner movement to concrete, historic engagement. *Both* sets of images are crucial and it is the dialectical holding-together of these images which is constitutive of Jaspers' idea of historicity. For historicity means that within the very concreteness and particularity of this (my) situation, and only in this concrete particularity, is Existenz as decisive ascending awareness of transcendence possible.

> Only in this appearance, not outside it in an imaginary detached self-being and an abstract transcendence, lies the present substance of what I am. This unity of mine with my phenomenal existence is my historicity.[39]

In contrast to an "imaginary detached self-being," then, Jaspers in effect is saying, "Look at how real people actually come to decisive self-realization and faith--not by some vague transcending, but by concrete decision made in personal quest and struggle, in real and ever particular situations and beliefs."

Jaspers tends not to identify his philosophy with one or several concrete historical persons, preferring rather to suggest an array of "great philosophers" and historic personages who have influenced his thinking and whose lives have exemplified various aspects of his thought. Still there is one person who may justly be said to serve here as an exemplary figure for Jaspers' idea of historicity--the Renaissance thinker Giordano Bruno whose life Jaspers contrasts with that of his more famous contemporary Galileo.[40] Both faced the same inquisitorial demand that they recant aspects of their writings. Galileo recanted and lived; Bruno refused and "died a martyr's death."[41] Jaspers exonerates Galileo since the truth in question was a matter of scientific knowledge which did not need the support of personal witness and which could (and would soon) be verified by countless others.

> A truth which I can prove stands without me;
> it is universally valid, unhistorical, timeless,
> but not absolute.[42]

Bruno's truth, however, was not a matter of knowledge, but of faith. It was truth attained in the arduous struggle of his personal history which would be realized only in the act of witness to that struggle and attainment.

> A truth by which I live stands only *if I become identical* with it; it is historical in form; as an objective statement it is not universally valid, but it is absolute.[43]

Thus Bruno is exemplary not because of the contents of his visionary thinking, however interesting they may be,[44] but because his life and above all his death show how the transcending faith of Existenz is attained only in concrete engagement, indeed only by actual identification with such particular contents.[45]

The intent of Jaspers' idea of historicity, then, is clear enough. Transcending faith not only does not preclude but actually demands engagement in and with concrete historic particularity as a fundamental condition of its possibility. Thus for Jaspers particularity is not something secondary, a mere occasion for existential historicity understood as the transcending movement of faith from some (thus any) particular point in time. Yet at this point it is still not clear why Jaspers affirms this and how he understands the relationship of absolute faith and historic relativity. Lest his talk of historicity and historic engagement seem an arbitrary assertion of will in the face of relativity (and thus no truth at all), or lest it seem an intellectual sleight of hand, a *tour de force* wherein the relative becomes suddenly, as if by magic, the bearer of absolute truth, it will be well to look a bit more closely at the dialectical pattern of Jaspers' understanding of historicity.[46]

As already noted, knowledge of history or a sense of history can set the stage for the historic self-realization of Existenz. But the awakening of Existenz is itself a free, personal act, not a conclusion from certain knowledge. Awareness of history's diversity (of religious diversity, for instance), of universal relativity and transience, may just as well lead to a variety of inauthentic attitudes.[47] Thus it is above all, Jaspers notes, concrete engagement in the world which opens the possibility of Existenz.

> Since I cannot become historic except by entering into existence, I cannot stay aloof from the world without losing my being as the realization of possible Existenz. In existence, as in particular concerns of existence, I need first to be involved at all....My involvement puts me into situations...and not until then can I experience what I want and act so as to become the historic phenomenon of my potential.[48]

Concrete involvement, in other words, opens the possibility of awareness of my personal reality as a reality in time, as a never-completed, historic struggle for realization in a situation which is itself historic. Such historic consciousness would grasp this situation from within, so to speak, not simply as a matter of objective interest, but as a matter of passionate personal concern. "In historic consciousness I know myself to be so identical with the particulars of my existence" that I understand them "as belonging to me in the more profound idea of my *fate*."[49]

I experience the boundary of historic situatedness, in other words, not as an experience of situatedness-in-general, but as a uniquely personal awakening to *this* historic particularity as *my* situation, as the possible medium of my realization. Such awakening is problematic, indeed threatening. It involves the loss of that secure harmony whereby one's situation (one's tradition, for instance, or one's religion) was naively identified as the whole.[50] It involves awareness of this situation as limited and particular--a mere speck on the vast panorama of history. Yet it is simultaneously awareness of this concrete reality as *my* historic possibility. It involves, then, both a distancing from the situation (a problematic awakening to oneself, to the mystery of one's freedom and destiny) and a tightening of the situation (by awareness of it as the reality of one's fate). In this experience of the boundary, when faced with the fundamental question about the ultimate significance or absurdity of one's life, one may receive assurance of transcendence in the unconditional action or faith of Existenz. Yet such transcending awareness of faith is here inseparable from "immersion in my historic definition" as the sole reality of my life.

> In this immersion I do not take up my fate as a merely external one, I take it up as mine; *amor fati*.... [Thus] the sense of historicity as a sense of fate means to take concrete existence seriously.[51]

Jaspers further clarifies this inseparability of transcending and concrete engagement in his discussion of communication. The idea of communication, in fact, is central to the theme of historicity.[52] Any historical action, of course, as the interaction of human beings, necessarily implies communication in some sense. Yet for Jaspers' thought communication is understood not simply as one characteristic of all historical activity, but as the primary and normative instance of that specific action wherein the awakening of Existenz in transcending faith remains always concrete and particular.

Communication, of course, is a complex phenomenon and not all communication involves the awakening and presence of Existenz. In fact such communication is rather rare and must be distinguished from ordinary communication as the pursuit of interests, the exchange of information, or the affirmation of ideas. In Jaspers' terminology, communication within the encompassing of Existenz must be distinguished from communication within the other modes of the encompassing (empirical existence, consciousness-at-large, and spirit), even though existential communication can only occur within the medium of these objective modes.[53] Binding together the diverse modes of communication as their common and fundamental motive is reason as the will to truth, and thus the will to unity and the will to communication. And it is this will to truth and unity which remains unsatisfied with the various immanent modes of human communication and thus pushes to their limits so that, at a given moment, in the give and take of ordinary communication, the possibility of a different kind of communication might arise.[54] In a discussion of religion, for instance (to move directly to the topic at issue here), whether in the on-going quest for reappropriation within a particular tradition or in the dialogue of different traditions, the discussion may approach certain limits where questions which are no longer matters of accurate knowledge or the ascertainment of ideas suddenly emerge with challenging clarity. The challenge may, of course, be avoided in the endless flow of information and ideas. Or it may be taken up as Existenz calls to Existenz. Then the reality of communication has changed, shifted, even though nothing has changed externally. Then the flow of information and the give and take of ideas become the medium of what Jaspers calls the "loving struggle" of Existenz with Existenz, of faith with faith.

Such existential communication can arise, then, only at the limits of other modes of communication when the quest for truth presses beyond those limits. It will not arise in the day to day "taken-for-grantedness" of one's faith, nor in the secure harmony of tradition, and not at all in the closed confines of exclusive orthodoxy.[55] As Jaspers says, "not until I cease to be so sheltered do I feel really impelled to communicate."[56] At the limit of such security--for instance in the present crisis where the harmony of tradition has been disrupted by doubt, by the awareness of relativity and the disturbing presence of other traditions--the possibility of such serious communicative quest for the truth arises. As always for Jaspers, experience of the boundary awakens Existenz. Yet (once again) the boundary is experienced not by some fantastic figure in brooding isolation, but concretely in the very real situation of human community and communication.

The encounter of such communication may, of course, take many forms and its contents will vary with the participants and the occasion or question which brings them together. (The dialogue of religions, however central to the present discussion, is just one example of a situation which might give rise to the loving struggle of communication.) Yet for Jaspers, such communication is not just one of many situations which might lead to the awakening of Existenz in boundary awareness and transcending faith. Rather, "it is *only* in communication that I come to myself."[57]

> The thesis of my philosophizing is: The individual cannot become human by himself. Self-being is only real in communication with another self-being. Alone, I sink into gloomy isolation--only in community with others can I be revealed in the act of mutual discovery.[58]

Communication is not just one way to truth, it is for Jaspers *the* way--the most fundamental condition, characteristic, and criterion of absolute truth.[59] For God, so to speak, or *sub specie aeternitatis*, truth may be final and one, but for men in time truth is manifold and developing--"indeed a truth developing in communication."[60]

Yet communication is the way to truth not in the sense that truth is the result attained *by means of* some special, esoteric ("existential") form of communication. Since the communication of Existenz with Existenz, in the medium of the ordinary communication of information and ideas, moves beyond the limits of those modes of communication, it does not share their results. It is rather a never completed process, whose only end is the possibility of fulfilled silence whence it will be taken up ever again.[61] Said differently, it ends only in failure to achieve results. Yet precisely this failure, this continual unfulfillment leads unpredictably to moments of transcending awareness, to awareness of transcendence as the ungraspable goal sought in communication, the unifying ground which unites the still divided participants and motivates the continuation of their struggle.

> The unfulfillment of communication and the difficulty of bearing its shipwreck become the revelation of a depth which nothing other than transcendence can fill.[62]

Thus absolute truth is attained, quite literally, *only in* (in the process of) communication and *not by means of* it. The struggle of communication, the movement to and fro of challenge and response, becomes itself the free and unconditional act (Existenz) of transcending faith.

In that endless give and take, however, the awareness of faith is never "hit upon at one stroke" (not attained as "an objective result that is held fast").[63] There is rather only "a moment's certainty" grasped, as it were, in bits and pieces, as hints and guesses which appear suddenly in the various turns of the conversation. Such awareness, moreover, "once it is not nothing to me, will appear to me as particular."[64] It will take form in the information and ideas, the particular beliefs and traditional views which are the content or substance of the dialogue and which become in the movement of communication momentarily transparent to or revelatory of transcendence.

> As existence tied to his tradition, the individual can only come to himself by adopting the expressive worlds he has inherited [even]if he adopts them to the end of a new original realization.[65]

Thus the attainment of the absolute truth of faith in communication is at once awareness of transcendence as that which encompasses oneself and the other, and a heightening of the particular form of that awareness as the reality of one's faith. In communication, in other words, one is thrown back upon oneself--in heightened awareness of the limit and particularity of one's situation (of one's tradition, for instance) vis à vis the other, yet simultaneously in awareness of this particularity as the reality of one's fate, and finally in adoption of this particularity as the realization of transcending faith. "Here I stand," so to speak, not forgetful of historic relativity and the presence of the other, not in arrogantly exclusive identification of my truth with transcendence, but in the realization that in time I can do nothing else. It is "here" only, albeit only in the movement of communication and in ever momentary (historic) attainment, that truth can be absolute (yet not exclusive).

Clearly, then, Jaspers' defense of particularity is not reducible to some (finally empty) choice of one particularity from among the range of possibilities thrown up by human history--as if one could calmly contemplate such possibilities from the outside, but then finally has to choose "because, after all, you can't stand every place at once." Truth would certainly be meaningless on such terms.[66] Nor is it equatable with those more sophisticated views in terms of which plurality is affirmed as part of a vision of the various cultures and religions, "each relating directly to God," each an inevitably historic and relative realization of transcendent faith.[67] There is no way in which this vision of the whole could be known as true. It is, moreover, despite its seductively harmonious character, finally destructive of that particular engagement whereby truth might actually be attained. Yet Jaspers' position is just as clearly not, at the other extreme, an absurd or historicist fatalism which finds the individual condemned to the prison of this particular situation. On the contrary, freedom, decision, choice are the crux of the matter for Jaspers:

> Truth is either cogent and thus not chosen, or it is made unconditional by choice.[68]

> Only as I am and do something unconditional in existence will transcendence also manifest itself to me....[69]

But it is not a choice from among diverse possibilities. This particularity for me "is not a possible *standpoint* that might be classified alongside other standpoints" for "as Existenz I cannot stand at my own back--something I can do quite well as consciousness at large."[70] When push comes to shove, so to speak, in concrete, communicative struggle the diversity of possibilities which can be known and (endlessly) reflected upon evaporates as I am challenged to declare myself. The choice, then, is a choice of myself, of the concrete reality of myself as Existenz in existence--"here I stand" for, in serious thought and communicative struggle, I cannot do otherwise.

> The choice I start from, as the source of existential truth, is the choice in which *Existenz chooses itself*. Instead of choosing a truth from the many types I am offered, I come to it by choosing the freedom of Existenz to elucidate itself in the world view that is true for it *alone*.[71]

It is not a passive resignation to fate, but an active love of my fate--"the truth of the *indissoluble union of particularity and Existenz* which we elucidate in the historic consciousness of *amor fati*."[72]

Active love of one's fate, then, is "the historic consciousness of *adopting* the particular as definition turned into the historic depth of Existenz itself."[73] It is the unconditional act whereby I take responsibility for my (real, concrete, existing) self--the free appropriation of this historic particularity which "becomes a function of possible Existenz" because "its contents and images point to me...appeal to me, challenge me...."[74] It is the deliberate decision to take myself in my concrete historic reality seriously, in fact to take this situatedness with unconditional seriousness.[75] It is the leap or shift whereby I am no longer simply an observer of my and other situatedness, nor simply "an individual finitely concerned with particular situations," but "infinitely concerned Existenz."[76]

Spoken of in terms of tradition, such adoption is not the naive "taken-for-grantedness" of those who live in the undisturbed unity of tradition, but that free reappropriation of tradition within the present crisis to which, as already noted, Jaspers' entire life's work was dedicated.[77] It is not a rigid, orthodox repetition of the past, nor "the desperate desolation of the 'well this is the way I am,'... [but] a deeper form of freedom [as] the choice of him who...takes himself over in his heritage, in this body, in this tradition."[78] It is, in other words, the rooting or replanting of freedom in the soil of history.[79] It permits or, rather, demands continuity and fidelity, for "the historicity of Existenz is its fidelity."[80] It both leads to and depends upon the "taken-for-grantedness" of everyday life and the community of life lived together under common authority.[81] And it is or can be such concrete and ordinary involvement in the ongoing life of a particular tradition and community (what Jean Wahl calls, paradoxically, a "relative catholicity"[82]) only because it is finally, unconditionally, taken to be true. In Jaspers' own words, "an Existenz adheres to its own traditional revelation of transcendence...in the particular form it has encountered and in the particular language...not on the ground that the revelation is one form of truth among others, that it is 'also true,' but because to Existenz this truth is truth pure and simple, the truth whereby its self-being will stand or fall."[83]

Yet, however much historic adoption demands continuity and fidelity, its truth is not the enduring possession of a known certitude.[84] It is, to reiterate the controlling idea of Jaspers' foundational thinking, not at all a matter of cognition or of objectivity. Objectively speaking (in terms of what can be known), one remains with historical relativities--the knowledge, for instance, that these beliefs have been held by this particular tradition in these ways at these times and places. To be sure, the shift occasioned by this limitation of knowledge opens the possibility of truth in historic adoption. But in that unconditional (existential) act truth is attained historically--in a moment, as fleeting awareness of transcendence in the struggle of communicative adoption.[85] It is, in Jaspers' frequently repeated metaphor, "truth in breakthrough" (*Wahrheit im Durchbruch*), in momentary realization which "cuts across time" (*quer zum Zeit*) as the "present eternity of Existenz."[86]

Historicity, then, is simultaneously (or dialectically) commitment to historic (enduring) particularity and historic (momentary) awareness of transcendence in (i.e., by means of and in the form of) that commitment. It is the unity in act, in a moment (and thus ever again to be re-enacted), of that which for thought remains inevitably dual.[87] To suggest this finally ineffable unity, Jaspers relies upon a continual flow of paradoxical formulations. Historic truth is the "appearance of transcendence," "the temporal manifestation of transcendence," or perhaps most aptly, "the vanishing presence of transcendence."[88] "The truth of historicity is the unity of temporality with the overcoming of time: it is the appearance of eternity."[89] Said again, it is the unity of "eternal being" and "evanescent phenomenon"--"not in the sense of a timeless validity that happens to be grasped now but would be just as capable of being grasped at some other time...but in the sense that, once fulfilled, the temporal particularity is comprehended as the appearance of eternal being...."[90] Yet because historic truth is attained only in "the factual moment deepened to present eternity," this attainment remains a "*tension-rich, never definitive realization.*"[91]

With such emphasis upon the historic/momentary character of existential truth, however, the critical questions about Jaspers' defense of particularity seem to return in full force. What of the actual, particular contents of such realization? Is their significance not diminished, and finally even negated by this emphasis (an emphasis which is, after all, not only unavoidable but clearly necessary in terms of Jaspers' foundational thinking)? To this challenge Jaspers (in what may here be considered the final clarification of his understanding of particularity) answers both "yes" and "no." The content or particular form of faith is at once nothing and everything--"infinitely important to the individual...and yet at the same time it is to him as nothing before transcendence."[92] "A sense of historicity," in other words, "can simultaneously lend absolute weight to existence...and keep it in suspension and relative, as mere existence."[93]

> The truth which Existenz acquires here in coming to itself is purely phenomenal, but the phenomenon as such, objectively conceived and held fast, is not the truth; it was true only because there was transcendence in it at the same time.[94]

The particular contents of faith, in other words, the ideas and beliefs, sacraments and rituals of my tradition, are what Jaspers calls "ciphers." What is adopted in existential historicity is adopted not as the objective (dogmatic or embodied) presence of transcendence, but as cipher. Or, more accurately, the objective becomes cipher of transcendence (becomes transparent to transcendence) in the unconditionality of historic adoption. As cipher ("because there was transcendence in it at the same time") it is "infinitely important to the individual."

The idea of cipher constitutes, of course, a major and, in some respects, a culminating theme in Jaspers' philosophy.[95] Thus his discussion of ciphers is both detailed and complex.[96] Yet in a real sense that discussion adds nothing substantially new to Jaspers' thought--to the idea, for instance, of faith and absolute truth. It is simply another of the different ways in which he approaches and thinks through his fundamental position. For the present, then, a brief reference to Jaspers' discussion of ciphers must suffice.

A first understanding of the idea of cipher can be suggested by reference to the basic philosophical operation discussed in the previous chapter.[97] Human consciousness remains always within the subject-object dichotomy. Awareness of transcendence, then, must occur within that dichotomy, in forms of objectivity. Yet this objective form of transcending awareness (or the concepts within which this awareness occurs) is "an objectivity which transcends all knowledge [and] thus not actually an object, but what we call cipher or symbol or metaphor."[98] It is awareness of transcendence in the form of objectivity attained precisely in the operation which moves in objectivity beyond it. Said differently, a cipher is the bearer of transcendence in the (finally not completable and thus endless) movement which negates its objectivity and keeps it "in suspension." Yet it is thus transparent to transcendence not in a merely speculative exercise of "formal transcending," but only if such thinking is one with the personal seriousness of Existenz ("the second wing"). In itself the cipher remains endlessly ambiguous. It is no longer a reality in the world as an object of knowledge, nor is it the reality of transcendence. "Ciphers are never the reality of transcendence itself, only its possible language."[99] Yet that language can be heard only by Existenz as it thinks "in the direction of transcendence," struggling to read the cipher language of its historic situation, and acts unconditionally, in historic adoption. In such moments, then, "the ciphers speak to us," "their glow will bear the message of transcendence," but "only on the premise that we keep them suspended while comprehending them in the depths to which we have access."[100]

For Jaspers, anything might thus become the "possible language of transcendence." Any thought, event, or object--an experience of nature, an encounter with history or with a living person, a poem or work of art, peaceful repose or extreme distress. All might become in a moment, for individual Existenz, "charged with the grandeur of God."[101] In a schematic ordering of the various realms of ciphers (or "languages of transcendence"), Jaspers refers to such immediate or intuitive experiences where suddenly one becomes attuned to the presence of transcendence as "the first language" or "the direct language of transcendence."[102] Such experience is unpredictable and might occur anywhere throughout human history and throughout an individual human life.[103] A sunrise, for instance, while known in scientific fact as no actual rising of the sun at all, might still in an historic moment serve realiably as language of transcendence.[104]

Yet even for the individual such experience leads directly to articulation as the effort to understand, and for humanity as a whole such articulation serves not only the quest for understanding but the necessary transmission of the initial experience from individual to individual and from generation to generation. Historically, according to Jaspers, such articulation first took concrete form as myth, religion, and art ("the second language") and later led to speculative reflection on these concrete articulations in various metaphysical categories and systems ("the third language").[105] The second and third languages, then, constitute what Jaspers calls "the world of ciphers," the various historic monuments and living traditions of those stories and images, events, rites, and beliefs, ideas and arguments in which human beings have thought and acted "in the direction of transcendence."[106] Thus while one may be uplifted by the first experience of transcendence in ciphers in the most startling and unforeseen ways, it is the world of ciphers, the second and third languages as they are concretely available in one's historic situation, and as they are taken up in historic adoption, which provide clarity and continuity for faith.

For Jaspers, then, while the world of ciphers is as vast as human history, all ciphers clearly are not equally possible languages for all men. Nor is what Jaspers calls "the reading of ciphers," the struggle of thinking and living in ciphers to hear the truth of transcendence, the same in each of the different realms of ciphers.[107] Clearly the way of the independent philosopher, wrestling with the heritage of great philosophical thought regardless of when or where it originated, is different from the more historically defined and communal path of the religious man.[108] In all cases, however, the contents of particular traditions (whether philosophical or religious) can be the possible language of transcendence *only for Existenz*, and then *only insofar as they are appropriated as ciphers* (i.e., only "on the premise that we keep them suspended").

> Transcendent reality, to be experienced by Existenz alone, is manifested in ciphers.[109]
>
> What speaks in ciphers is not heard by any intellect... [but] only by the freedom of Existenz with which transcendence communicates in that language.[110]

Thus the fundamental perversion of ciphers occurs not when the cipher world is simply observed as a phenomenon of human history. As such, in the study of religions, for instance, particular ciphers become quite legitimate objects of historical knowledge. Rather ciphers are perverted when, in Jaspers' terms, they are regarded as "embodied transcendence"--as a definite grasp (known or revealed) of transcendence in this particular object of perception or thought.[111] Such definite attainment of transcendence is clearly impossible in terms of the foundations of Jaspers' thought. (Being-in-itself does not appear in the subject-object dichotomy; what appears is always particular or phenomenal being.) If, then, "the reality of transcendence is thus captured...we have lost transcendence."[112] And the possibility of Existenz as the only way to the real truth of transcendence has also been lost. For the only appropriate response to embodied transcendence is blind (idolatrous) obedience and authoritative preservation in fixed (dogmatic) form. Yet in such form the cipher language grows silent, its light darkened. "Any fixation would extinguish them. To stay alive they must remain suspended."[113] For it is precisely as suspended, as not objectively definite but ambiguously aglow with possible depth, that they appeal not to knowing consciousness but to possible Existenz. Jesus as *the* incarnate God is intellectual nonsense and a religious offense, but as unique cipher of God's presence to man and man's to God the figure of Jesus and christological doctrine provide an immense depth of possible truth.[114] The truth of the cipher will speak, however, only to Existenz in its struggle to plumb that depth, and even then its truth will never be attained unambiguously and finally, but only historically.

Ciphers, then, when not proclaimed as definite truth to be learned and obeyed, call to that in man which moves beyond the limits of the secure and knowable. They invite participation in what Jaspers calls "the twofold struggle"--the struggle, against our own (idolatrous) hunger for secured objectivity, to keep the ciphers suspended by the endlessly dialectical negation of their objectivity, and the subsequent communicative struggle ("in the realm of ciphers") of interpretation against interpretation, cipher against cipher.[115] In the movement of these two, inseparable struggles (as, for instance, in the quest for the truth of a particular religion or in the dialogue of religions), particular ciphers may become, historically, the language of transcendence.

It is clear, then, that Jaspers' discussion of ciphers recapitulates the basic aspects of his defense of particularity. The contents of a particular faith may be appropriated only as ciphers, but the cipher language of transcendence can be heard only in particular, historic appropriation. *Ciphers are as such always particular* (and plural). The language of transcendence speaks not everywhere, not through "ciphers-in-general," but in the language of this particular cipher heard in the historic and communicative struggle for its truth. The reading of particular ciphers, in other words, is accomplished by "adoptive interpretation." And in such reading, "the interpreter does not come close to them until he lives them (*in ihnen mitlebt*)."[116] Ciphers, then, are not (objective, embodied) mediators of transcendence, but they do mediate the "forever new immediacy" of existential awareness of transcendence.[117]

3.

The third, and final, aspect of Jaspers' response to the type of criticism outlined at the end of the preceding chapter concerns the adequacy of his account of historic particularity for the understanding of *religious* truth. Given that this account of particularity does permit (in Jaspers' view) a significant plurality, is it adequate as an account of religious plurality and thus as the basis for an affirmation of the possibility of a plurality of true religions?

Here the essence of Jaspers' response can be put quite briefly (it is a qualified, yet definite "yes"), because Jaspers really takes very little time to argue the question. The bulk of his discussion of religion, as already suggested at various points in the preceding pages, consists of an extensive, rather repetitive critique of religious self-understanding on the grounds that it constitutes an idolatrous fixation or embodiment of transcendence and that, consequently, it becomes an authoritarian negation of freedom (Existenz) as the sole authentic path to transcendent truth.[118] Correspondingly much of the discussion of Jaspers from religious quarters has focused on the inaccuracy of his critique of religion. Indeed it is difficult for a religious person to recognize his own belief and practice in Jaspers' at times tiresome rehearsal of standard Enlightenment and liberal attacks on religion as superstitious materialization of the divine and slavish obedience to narrowly dogmatic authorities.[119] All too often, in fact, Jaspers betrays what seems surprising ignorance of actual religions and their many specific differences.[120] Jaspers, of course, might well respond that it is the (academic and predominantly liberal) theologians who are out of touch with the reality of religion as it is lived by the masses. Yet the theologians could in turn respond that the critique of what is idolatrous in popular religion has been and remains a primary concern of authentic religion.[121]

Yet the thrust and parry of such exchange is, for present purposes at least, really somewhat beside the point--as the continual return to and even fascination with Jaspers by religious thinkers would seem to suggest.[122] Indeed what is most surprising about much religious commentary on Jaspers, in light of his persistent attacks, is the lack of concern to spend much time and space responding to this negative critique and the evident concern to test the viability of his proffered alternative.[123] And this, far from constituting a failure to take Jaspers seriously, is actually quite in accord with his intentions since, as already noted, the goal of his discussion of religion is "to promote truth in religion by means of a philosophical critique." The purpose of his constantly repeated attacks is to enable the churches to crack "the shells of their dogmas and institutions and find in them a contemporary voice."[124] If religious believers no longer recognize themselves in his critique, then so be it! Perhaps the necessary transformation of religious self-understanding is already underway and religious truth is increasingly understood by religious men in terms approaching Jaspers' own.

Thus the real issue is not whether Jaspers' negative critique of religion is accurate, but whether his positive prescriptions are adequate. At least for the topic under discussion here, the question is whether his analysis of truth as historicity (and thus as particularity and plurality) is adequate as an understanding of religious truth. And Jaspers' answer, as noted, is a straightforward, albeit qualified, affirmative.

For Jaspers, in fact, the real question is not whether his analysis of truth fits the actuality of the religions, but whether the religions for their own survival can be transformed so as to fit the conditions of truth made inescapable by the present crisis--and that, for him, inevitably means transformation according to the understanding of truth outlined in his writings.[125] Jaspers does not want boldly to claim that his writings must now become the norm in terms of which the canons of the great religions are to be interpreted.[126] One of the first qualifications he makes regarding his position is that the required transformation of the religions must be accomplished from within, by virtue of their own dynamism, as religious persons struggle in the present crisis to return to the "primal source" of their own traditions.[127] The philosopher, who stands on the outside, "cannot possibly tell the theologians and the churches what to do," but he can help to "prepare the ground and...produce awareness of the intellectual situation necessary for the growth of what he himself cannot create," and he can raise "questions that he cannot answer, though he knows that the future will assuredly give the answer."[128] In his "loving struggle" with religious believers, moreover, he cannot but assert what he believes to be true--that faith must be transformed according to the basic conditions made inescapable in our day and clarified via foundational thinking.

Thus while specifics of the necessary change in religious self-understanding are generally not discussed by Jaspers, the broad lines of such change are clear and can be summarized by the statement that the contents of each religious tradition must be reappropriated as ciphers.[129] Speaking specifically to the religious situation in the West, Jaspers briefly suggests the significance of this change for "biblical religion."[130] It is, he stresses, "not the substance of the biblical faith that needs transforming, but its appearance...its garb."[131] Yet this change must nonetheless be "a change as far-reaching as all the other changes that have taken place in our era--or else the eternal truth of biblical religion will recede beyond the horizon of man--and it is impossible to say what might take its place."[132] It means a change in one's appropriation of the Bible--from divinely inspired book (the idea of revelation must itself be understood as a cipher[133]) to a compilation of "a thousand years of religious, mythical, historic, and existential experience," a rich record of embattled, conflicting ciphers which invites and requires historic adoption.[134] Thus, too, the person Jesus cannot literally be taken as the God-man, but as a magnificent cipher of the legitimacy of ciphers (mediators between God and man) and of man's inexpressible closeness to God.[135] More generally, then, the claims to dogmatic and exclusive truth must be abandoned so that the eternal truth of the tradition might be "retrieved from fixations" by the historic penetration and adoption of its contents as ciphers.[136]

Yet this call for the transformation of the religions would seem to raise again the basic question about the religious adequacy of Jaspers' understanding of truth. Does not the transformation of particular religious contents into ever-ambiguous ciphers ("mere ciphers") negate the positivity which Jaspers himself regards as the distinguishing characteristic of religion? Does it not in effect destroy the basic religious passions of reverence and (communal) worship, replacing them with (individual) philosophic contemplation and existential decision? In Jaspers' own words, "If we deny embodiment of the divine, are we not sloughing off everything sacramental?"[137] In response, Jaspers would admit the risk involved in this transformation, but would argue that precisely this risk might call forth the earnestness or seriousness of faith in adoptive interpretation. Authentic faith, in other words, must run the risk of freedom.[138] Only in freedom does sacramentalism "not lure us into those embodying traps," yet in freedom, "ritualism and sacramentalism are possible in a life with ciphers."[139] The transformation of positive religious contents into ciphers, then, does not for Jaspers destroy their positivity and particularity. Rather it "retrieves them from fixations," making their authentic appropriation in faith a real possibility while at the same time preserving them from the type of reductionism which is involved, for instance, in Bultmann's disastrous program of demythologizing.[140]

For Jaspers, then, not only is his understanding of truth as historic adoption of ciphers religiously adequate, it is in fact absolutely necessary as the basis for that reappropriation of religious faith which is required in the present crisis. It provides that "common framework so broadly based that historically heterogeneous faiths could communicate in it without abandoning themselves" and "could transform themselves by their own depth... into the new foundations that human seriousness needs under the conditions of the coming age."[141] It opens the possibility of a future not of facile tolerance (which is really indifference), but of the loving struggle of communication in real tolerance.

"For authentic truth arises only where faiths meet in the presence of the encompassing."[142] Thus it opens the possibility, for the first time, of a real unity of mankind--not via an unrealizable universal faith, "but in boundless communication of the historically different in never-ending dialogue, rising to heights of noble emulation."[143]

Such, then, is Jaspers' controlling vision of religious plurality and truth, and his corresponding claim that the religions must be transformed in terms of that vision. Once again, of course, Jaspers qualifies this claim--not only, as already noted, by stressing that this transformation can be accomplished only from within the churches, but by admitting that finally, after every effort at comprehension, religion remains the uncomprehended other which stands in polar opposition to philosophy. The philosopher cannot but articulate the claims which thought seems to render inescapable, yet he too finally speaks in ciphers and in faith and must remain open to the otherness of the religious world which escapes his grasp.[144] Yet while such qualification is undoubtedly truthful on Jaspers' part, it is not particularly significant for the present discussion. What is significant is the adequacy of the idea of religious truth proposed by Jaspers, however gently that proposal is made at certain times. The following chapter will attempt to evaluate that adequacy.

V.

CRITICISM

Up to this point in the present work I have tried as much as possible to let Jaspers speak with his own voice (just as, in the introductory chapter, I attempted to present the problem as it is understood in much contemporary thinking). Interpretation, of course, is inevitable especially in the type of summary argument presented in the preceding chapters. Yet the direction, the sequence of issues raised, and the various twists and frequent repetitions in the argument have been an attempt to represent the direction and the twisting, repetitive movement characteristic of Jaspers' thinking. My own comments have been limited to remarks in various footnotes and questions raised at the end of Chapters II and III. In the present chapter, however, I shall try to develop the criticism of Jaspers which is either stated or implied in those notes and questions in order to evaluate the adequacy of his proposed resolution to the problem of religious pluralism and truth.

The primary purpose of this concluding chapter, then, is to answer the question, "Does Jaspers succeed in providing a way of understanding religious truth so that more than one religion may strictly speaking be said to be true?" As indicated at the very beginning of this study, the question is answered in the negative since Jaspers' resolution to the problem of religious pluralism and truth is found wanting. Yet his thought is also taken to be typical or representative of much contemporary thinking about the problem which builds upon fundamentally similar foundations and moves in the same direction or within the same basic framework.[1] Thus a secondary and more general purpose of both the preceding analysis and the present critique is to understand Jaspers' thinking (and by implication the type of thinking it represents) in order to understand why, despite much that seems promising, it nonetheless goes wrong. Why is it, in other words, that a thinking which contains many of the elements of what would seem to constitute an adequate analysis of religious truth in a context of religious pluralism somehow still fails to bring these various pieces of the puzzle together in an adequate way? An answer to that question, although far from being a resolution of the problem of pluralism and truth, might at least suggest different and hopefully more adequate directions for thought about the problem.

Yet the difficulty of any attempt to develop a serious critique of Jaspers' thinking has already been noted. Because his work attempts to deal systematically with the deeper currents of modern thought, it takes one to the center of today's most fundamental and controversial issues. Thus a fully adequate critique can finally flow only from an equally clear and fundamental position as regards those issues. In the absence of such a position, one runs the risk of merely stringing together comment after comment without any real unity and without any assurance of having touched the crucial or fundamental point. The ideal requirements of criticism, then, place serious strains upon the practical limitations of time and space, to say nothing of those more significant limitations imposed by the critics' own want of wit and wisdom. For all these difficulties, however, the primary focus of the following critique remains the question of the adequacy of Jaspers' understanding of religious truth as it purports to resolve the problems posed by contemporary consciousness of religious pluralism. Insofar as discussion of that question inevitably involves more fundamental issues, those issues will be taken up--without, however, any claim that they will have been adequately or thoroughly discussed.

Thus after (1) a brief, introductory section on the way in which the critique of Jaspers will be approached, (2) discussion will focus upon the failure of Jaspers' thought to account for the religious plurality it intends to affirm, and thus his failure to clarify the logic whereby a plurality of religions could be equally true. A concluding section (3) will explore the reasons for this failure and attempt to draw out implications for a more adequate understanding of religious plurality and truth.

1.

One of the ways in which a critique of Jaspers' discussion of religious pluralism might be developed is exemplified by the type of argument made (at least implicitly) in much theological writing.[2] From within the context of one particular religion, the theologians basically argue that Jaspers in effect solves the problem only by dissolving it. His call for the transformation of the religions is understood not as a change *in* religion, but as a change *of* the religions into something else, into a general philosophical faith. It removes the stumbling block, the concrete particularity of origin and tradition characteristic of religious faith, and thereby removes the very point at which the various religions are most different (and whence other differences, above all oppositions of doctrine, flow). For it is clear that Judaism, Christianity, and Islam (at least as traditionally understood) originated in and continue to stand (or fall) by the truth of what Emil Fackenheim has recently called "root experiences" of God's presence and action in history.[3] It is equally clear that the origin of other religions in historical events, founders, and scriptures which are taken to be revelatory (even if the relation of the divine and history is not understood as it is in biblical religion) likewise establishes the basis of their distinctiveness and may well, then, constitute "the largest difficulty in the way of religious agreement."[4] Thus when Jaspers would transform the understanding of such concrete, revelatory origins (and of the doctrine which flows from them) into ciphers of human transcending, he would change not something accidental, but something essential to the actuality of the religions and to their diversity. To put the matter more generally, by means of that type of symbolic understanding of religion which has today become widespread, the real differences among the religions are in effect negated and the "problem of pluralism" is resolved--that is, shown to be really no problem at all.[5]

In response to such criticism Jaspers would, I think, reiterate (at least) two of the central points made in his discussion of religious truth.[6] In the first place, he would continue to maintain that attention to the new realities of our age (as articulated in critical philosophy) simply makes a transformation of traditional religious self-understanding inescapable. Truth demands that sacred origins, revelations, and doctrines be reappropriated today as ciphers of transcendence. Any other less critical understanding of religious traditions is no longer tenable. Secondly, however, and more positively, he would argue that while the appropriation of religious origins and beliefs as ciphers may seem like the dissolution of all particularity when viewed from within the fortress of orthodoxy, it in fact constitutes the only possible and still very real affirmation of particularity, and thus of plurality. He would, in other words, vigorously reject the charge that his call for the transformation of the religions results in a loss of the concrete particularity of the various religions and thus of their differences and real opposition.

While Jaspers would, of course, conclude his rebuttal with the standard caveat that for him religious faith finally remains inexplicably other, he would also repeat his complaint that "discussion with theologians always breaks off at the crucial point. They fall silent...assert something unconditionally... and in the last analysis they are not really interested. For in the last analysis they are certain of their truth, terrifyingly certain."[7] The theologians, in reply, would find Jaspers' brand of tolerance to be likewise terrifyingly certain, closed, and dogmatic. Thus the argument seems to get nowhere as Jaspers and the theologians talk past each other, each from within a set position. The theologians base their critique on the actuality of religious faith. Jaspers replies that while he knows what the religions actually are it is that actuality which must be changed and can be changed without destroying religious particularity.

However valid, then, the theological critique of Jaspers' discussion of pluralism and truth (and I find myself fundamentally in agreement with it), it probably does not provide the best avenue of approach for a critical understanding of Jaspers' ideas. The adequacy of Jaspers' position can perhaps be better evaluated, and the reasons for its inadequacy more clearly understood, not by a critique which originates within the particularity of religious faith (and thus "from outside" Jaspers' thought), but by an approach which seeks to evaluate Jaspers on his own terms, to develop a critique "from within" his own position. Such, at any rate, is the approach taken here.[8]

The basic argument of this critique from within is that there is not simply a gap, but actually a contradiction between intention and performance whereby key aspects of Jaspers' performance negate or undercut those other aspects of his thought which are crucial for the intended affirmation of religious particularity and plurality. To put the matter in slightly different terms, there is, as already noted,[9] a pervasive ambiguity or tension in Jaspers' thinking such that what he gives, so to speak, with one hand he takes back with the other. What he intends to affirm and argues persuasively for at certain points he then not only fails to sustain but actually negates at other points in his arguments.

It has already been suggested that this fundamental tension might be understood historically as a basic irreconcilability between the older traditions and the new conditions within which Jaspers would reappropriate them.[10] Yet it can be even more clearly understood in terms of the general dialectical structure of Jaspers' thinking. For at various levels and in different ways the structure of that thinking consists of a continual "holding together" of polar or opposed elements--past traditions with new conditions, and more specifically (for present purposes) limitation, mediation, and concrete particularity with break-through, immediacy, and transcendence. It is this structure which necessitates the continual movement characteristic of Jaspers' thinking and which thus opens the possibility of that (non-cognitive) act of transcending which is its real center. Yet it is, I think, this very structure, or its failure, which does not simply illustrate but is in fact the basis of the pervasive and destructive tension in Jaspers' thought. For while Jaspers intends this structure as a continual holding-together of polar elements (dialectic understood as endless movement, circling and suspension), it becomes in reality the means whereby the various elements of one side of the polarity are effectively taken over and transformed by the other side (dialectic as negation and transformation). In the specific case of religious truth, then, while Jaspers intends to hold together historic particularity and transcending faith, or mediation and immediacy, so that religious particularity (and plurality) can be affirmed even within modern critical consciousness, the actual if unintended result of his thinking is that all particular mediations are transformed and effectively negated by a more fundamental emphasis on immediacy.[11]

The critique from within, then, is essentially that there is in Jaspers' thinking a contradiction between intention and performance such that he fails to establish a logical basis for the affirmation of a possible plurality of true religions, and that this failure is rooted in a basic antagonism between conflicting elements of his own thinking. At this point, however, the critique has been merely asserted, not argued. Thus a more detailed review of specific aspects of Jaspers' thinking is needed. The central issue, of course, continues to be Jaspers' account of religious particularity--whether his understanding of religious truth, and the dialectical logic upon which that understanding is based, does or does not sustain the possibility of religious particularity and thus the possibility of religious differences, real oppositions, and a real plurality of true religions. For the basic question under discussion in this dissertation is not, to repeat, a substantive question concerning the truth of Jaspers' existential affirmation of transcendence any more than it is a substantive question about the truth or falsity of the claims made by particular religions. The question throughout has been, rather, a logical one. Does Jaspers provide an understanding of truth in religion which reconciles the requirements of an adequate idea of truth with the exigencies of contemporary consciousness of religious pluralism (i.e., with irreducible differences or real oppositions, and the possibility of a plurality of equally true religions)? The following critique is an attempt to show that he does not--that the logic of his idea of existential truth, while it does allow a certain, indeed an inevitable sense of plurality, effectively negates that stronger or more problematic sense of plurality whence the original question of plurality and truth arises. He does this, moreover, contrary to what is intended and explicitly affirmed in his idea of existential truth, by undercutting the account of religious particularity which is basic to that stronger sense of pluralism.[12]

2.

Since intention and performance are the operative categories for this critique, I should begin with a brief restatement of Jaspers' intention before attempting to show how it is betrayed by the destructive tension between key aspects of his performance. As already noted, the importance of Jaspers' discussion derives in part at least from the fact that he understands the question of religious pluralism and truth within the broader context of the crisis of our age and thus as a political question of immense significance.[13] It is his conviction that in this crisis the future of our humanity depends not upon some wholesale embrace of technology accompanied, perhaps, by romantic visions of a great leap beyond the ruins of the present towards a global future and a new, universal faith. Yet neither does it depend upon a desperate clinging to past orthodoxies. Rejecting both alternatives, Jaspers stresses that a truly human *and* truly global future depends, rather, upon the possibility of contemporary reappropriation of the great religious traditions *in their concrete diversity*. In the broadest sense, then, the intention of his discussion of religion is to provide a logical basis for that contemporary reappropriation, one which would at once rescue the traditional faiths from the sclerosis into which they have sunken and simultaneously provide a framework for their mutual recognition and intercommunication. Thus in terms of the specific issue of pluralism and truth his intention is to provide an understanding of the logic of religious truth which makes possible a strong affirmation of the truth of one's particular faith without the concomitant claim to its normative or exclusive character. Or, to put the matter more positively, his intention is to provide a basis, within contemporary consciousness of pluralism, for an absolute commitment to the truth of one religious particularity which simultaneously allows the possible truth (in an identical sense) of other particular faiths.

The performance whereby Jaspers seeks to realize this intention is, of course, the whole of that extended and systematic thinking which has been recapitulated in the preceding chapters. For present purposes, however, the core of that performance can be indicated in terms of Jaspers' account of the logic of religious truth as an existential logic--a logic which, in direct contrast to the logic of cognitive truth, *must always be historic and particular and, while necessarily absolute, can never be universal and exclusive*. For the movement at the center of this logic, a movement at once of thought and of freedom arises only at the limits of cognitive truth where the security of universal claims must be abandoned. Only in the absence of exclusive cognitive claims is there the possibility of that shift in subjectivity which constitutes an awakening in basic or unconditional trust, a coming to oneself as Existenz which is simultaneously an awareness of transcendence. Yet Jaspers insists, as we have seen, that this existential awakening occurs not in abstracted isolation, but in concrete or historical struggle within one's real situation. It leads to truth only insofar as it leads to particular commitment, to what Jaspers describes as adoption or the personal appropriation of an always particular faith. Such truth is existential, then, not simply because it is truth of and for life, truth which "counts for the whole of one's life," but because it is truth attained and affirmed only in passionately engaged living. It is, in the standard cliché, not a matter of dispassionate objectivity, but of pathos and participation, and thus of particularity.

For Jaspers, moreover, this necessarily particular yet non-exclusive logic of religious truth is dictated not only by the nature of religious subjectivity, but also by the reality of the object which it affirms.[14] For that object, which Jaspers prefers to speak of simply as "transcendence," cannot be an object of knowledge and thus can neither be known nor revealed in any universally valid way. Yet as the object or content of religious truth, transcendence must still be made present or revealed *to* human life--conceived in the categories of human thought and concretized in the forms of human action. In Jaspers' terms, the language of transcendence must be mediated through the language of ciphers, that multiform world of myth and story, parable and paradox, abstract doctrine and sacramental form which makes up the content of the different traditions of religious (and philosophical) faith. The truth of transcendence, however, is not simply present ("embodied" would be Jaspers' term) in the contents of the traditions so that their various truth claims might all be affirmed as equally true. (On the contrary, it is the clear oppositions among these truth claims which gives rise to the problem of pluralism and truth in the first place.) Truth is revealed or attained, rather, only insofar as the traditional contents, understood as ciphers, are taken up and transformed in that dialectical process which Jaspers speaks of as "adoptive interpretation." It is, in other words, only as part of the personal and communicative struggle to be faithful to, yet to wrestle with and to live into the truth of ever particular beliefs (or contents) that they might mediate historically the truth of transcendence. The language of transcendence, then, is spoken only in particular languages or ciphers. In such particularity the truth which is heard is absolutely true, yet the speaking and hearing is such that it cannot be taken as universally or normatively true, but must admit the possibility of other, even of opposed truths.

Once again, then, the existential logic clarified by Jaspers' discussion is such that religious truth must always be particular and thus can, it would seem, admit of real plurality. Thus Jaspers' performance with its central emphasis upon and its specific understanding of the necessary particularity of all religious truth claims would seem to be perfectly consistent with his intentions. For it is on the basis of this existential understanding of religious truth that he rejects not only orthodox exclusivity, but also that type of pervasive relativism which reduces the plurality of religions to so many culturally specific symbol systems. And it is on the same basis that he dismisses those easy visions of the progressive convergence of the world religions, emphasizing rather his own hope for the continued "loving struggle" of divergent faiths. Thus while one might well disagree with the content of that analysis, it does not seem possible, at least at this point, to fault his performance for its failure to sustain his intentions. On the contrary, it is the centrality of emphasis upon historicity and particularity which most seems to recommend Jaspers' proposed resolution to the problem of pluralism and truth.

Yet, as suggested above, what Jaspers gives (or seems to give) with one hand he takes back with the other and it is precisely this central and crucial emphasis on particularity which his performance fails in the end to sustain. For on closer examination in terms of the full and dialectical framework of Jaspers' thought his continual affirmations of the necessary particularity of religious truth are not quite what they seem to be or, more significantly, are not what they must be if they are to provide a basis for the affirmation of a possible plurality of true religions. To put the matter in different terms, for Jaspers, as we have seen, particular religious claims might be affirmed as true only insofar as they are understood dialectically. Jaspers, of course, is not alone in stressing the necessity of a dialectical appropriation of religious language.[15] Yet what he means by a dialectical understanding of particular claims, or the character and context of the dialectical appropriation which he calls for, is quite specific. And it is, I submit, his specific dialectical understanding of religious truth which not only fails to sustain but actually undercuts the central emphasis on particularity which is so crucial for the intended affirmation of a possible plurality of true religions.

I can perhaps best begin to argue this contention by reiterating that the fundamental tenet, so to speak, of the logic of religious truth proposed by Jaspers is not simply that truth is attained only via historic adoption, but that such adoption involves a process of adoptive interpretation. It involves, in other words, a *transformation* of the particular contents of belief whereby they are appropriated as ciphers. Thus the particular contents of belief are kept dialectically suspended so that they might serve as vehicles for the free transcending of Eixstenz and thereby mediate the authentic language of transcendence. But what, it must be asked, is the significance of this transformation for that particularity which has been so strongly affirmed as central to the logic of religious truth? In what sense does religious truth remain particular within this dialectic of adoptive interpretation? Or, to put the central question here more directly, if the problem of pluralism and truth arises because the specific contents or claims of particular faiths are opposed, do such particular oppositions remain once the contents of faith have been appropriated as ciphers? If they do not--if, in other words, Jaspers' thought fails to sustain the strong sense of particularity upon which such opposition is based--then in a real sense he may be said not to have resolved the problem of pluralism and truth but to have dissolved it. For if particular religious faiths might be true, yet not in terms of those specific contents whereby they stand opposed to other faiths, then while there would still be a plurality of particular faiths, there would be no problem of pluralism and truth. A plurality of religions could be true simply as so many accidentally (i.e., historically) divergent ways of expressing the same truth or, alternatively, as so many necessary, but again only accidentally different occasions for the affirmation of that (one) truth which transcends them all.

At the risk of being repetitious, I should perhaps sharpen the issue here by delineating more explicitly two quite different senses in which particularity might be affirmed in the discussion of religious pluralism. In the first and, I think, stronger sense, the idea of particularity refers to the particular *contents* of a given faith--to the particularity of the "root experience" or revelatory events at the origin of that faith and of the specific ritual forms and doctrinal claims which flow from that origin. When this first sense of particularity is involved in the assertion that a particular faith is true, it means that the particular contents of that faith are true--however much those contents cannot be taken literally or dogmatically or magically; however much, that is, they must be dialectically negated as well as affirmed in the adoptive struggle to live into their truth. It means, to use Jaspers' terms, that these contents in their particularity mediate the truth of transcendence. By way of a convenient shorthand, then, this first sense of particularity could be referred to as mediatory particularity or *particularity as mediation*. In the second sense, the idea of particularity refers to the fact that human life must unavoidably be lived in some particular situation, and human thought necessarily involves some particular contents. Thus the attempt of religious faith to think about and to live in relation to transcendence is unavoidably or necessarily particular. The transcending movement of faith can only occur in the context of certain particular contents. When this second sense of particularity is involved in the assertion that a particular faith is true, it means that the particular contents of that faith serve as the context or vehicle or springboard for that transcending movement precisely insofar as those contents are dialectically "transformed" (i.e., negated in their particularity). Said again, the particular faith is true not by virtue of the particularity of its contents, but by virtue of the *function* they play as an occasion for transcending. A convenient shorthand for this second sense of particularity, then, might be *particularity as occasion.*

Now religious pluralism could be understood in terms of either of these senses of particularity since the affirmation of either would necessarily involve a possible plurality of religions. As noted above, however, the problem of religious pluralism and truth arises in terms of the first sense of particularity. Thus the attempt to resolve that problem by affirming, with Jaspers, that more than one religion can strictly be said to be true must likewise involve this stronger sense of particularity.[16]

The "defense of particularity" outlined in the previous chapter is, of course, Jaspers' effort to sustain such a strong affirmation of particularity within the transformation required by his existential logic. And that defense does indeed establish the necessity or inevitability of historic particularity as the medium of transcending faith. As part of that defense, moreover, Jaspers argues strenuously against the objection that it is simply particularity as such (particularity as occasion) and thus any particularity and nothing really particular (i.e., as *this* particular) that counts. He speaks movingly of the richness of specific traditions and of the necessity of the type of concrete adoption exemplified by the "Here I stand" of figures like Giordino Bruno. While he demands the transformation of the contents of particular traditions and commitments into ciphers, he repeatedly stresses the necessary particularity of all ciphers and the fact that the truth of faith can be attained only in ever specific ciphers. Yet for all the inevitability of historic particularity, the argument for the significance of the particular in terms of the unique particularity of its contents (particularity as mediation), and thus as something significantly different and not simply an instance of a general necessity--this argument fails.

Take, for instance, the exemplary significance for Jaspers' understanding of truth of a figure like Bruno. It can be argued on historical grounds, I believe, that what was important for Bruno, so important that he was willing to die for it, was the truth in which he believed--the truth, that is, of the content of his belief. The same could also be said of other exemplary figures like Thomas More and Luther. To put the matter graphically, the fundamental accent in a "Here I stand" uttered by any of these men would be upon the word "Here" (i.e., with this conviction) regardless of how much emphasis might also be placed upon the word "I." Yet for Jaspers the significance of Bruno--and the significance of More and Luther for those others who have recently turned to them in a similar way--is not the truth of the content of his belief, even when that content is understood dialectically as cipher, but the truth of the form of that believing. In terms of the idea of particularity exemplified by Jaspers' use of Bruno, then, what is affirmed is not the particular content of Bruno's belief (which has long since become a curiosity for the history books), but the fact and form of his believing--not the "what" but the "how." That "how," of course, for all three figures necessarily involved grappling with and affirming particular contents. Yet the particularity is true not because of those particular contents (as *mediators*) but because those contents happened to be the locus (or *occasion*) for the movement of existential faith. In terms of the question of pluralism, then, while the content of what Bruno and Luther and More affirmed (as regards, say, the authority of the papacy) is not just different but in clear opposition, their significance is the same and so too, finally, is their truth (as Existenz in relation to transcendence), even if that truth could actually be attained only in the historic adoption of particular and divergent contents.

The point here can perhaps be made more clearly in terms of Jaspers' notion of cipher. Just as his defense of particularity could be recapitulated by reference to his discussion of ciphers, so too the inadequacy of that defense can be seen in that discussion. For what, it must be asked, is the truth of a cipher, or in what sense might a particular cipher be affirmed as true? As just indicated with reference to Bruno's beliefs, such an affirmation might be made not by virtue of a cipher's contents, although admittedly there would be no cipher to affirm without particular contents, but by virtue of its function. In fact the very idea of ciphers refers not to some special category of beliefs but to an action or function--to a way of relating to particular beliefs or better yet, to a way of relating to transcendence by means of particular beliefs.[17] Certain beliefs, then, might be true *when appropriated as ciphers*. That is to say they are true not as an adequate expression, however paradoxically or dialectically understood, of religious reality as revealed, say, in the "root experience" of some particular faith. They are true, rather, only insofar as they function as a vehicle or occasion for the movement of existential transcending, or, to change the language somewhat, only insofar as they serve to mediate the immediacy of Existenz as non-cognitive awareness of transcendence.[18] They serve this function, moreover, or they are appropriated as ciphers, precisely insofar as their particular content is transformed by being brought into suspension or negated. Thus while noting that the contents of traditional beliefs "used to impress men as true reality," Jaspers stresses:

> When we say "ciphers," we expressly do not mean to refer to things, matters, facts, realities, although it seems that cipher contents have mostly been viewed as realities....The great step in which man transforms himself occurs...when the contents that have been conceived and visualized are stripped of objective reality.[19]

To put the matter in terms of the basic "subject-object dichotomy" framework of Jaspers' thought, it is only by means of the continual effort to move beyond or through the object "in the direction of transcendence" that the object becomes a cipher. The contents of a particular belief, then, could be affirmed as true insofar as they function as ciphers, and they can function as ciphers insofar as they are caught up in the dialectical process which negates their objectivity and keeps them in suspension.[20]

The idea of cipher, then, is at the heart of Jaspers' affirmation of particularity. There is no cipher without particular contents and without the historic adoption of those contents. Thus Jaspers can, as we have seen, affirm the truth of those contents:

> An Existenz adheres to its own traditional revelation of transcendence...in the particular form it has encountered and in the particular language...not on the ground that the revelation is one form of truth among others, that it is "also true," but because to Existenz this truth is truth pure and simple, the truth whereby its self-being will stand or fall.[21]

Here once again, however, the meaning of this very strong affirmation of particularity is not quite what it at first seems to be (and it will not carry the weight which Jaspers intends it to carry). When understood in terms of Jaspers' basic dialectic, what seems the quite straightforward meaning of his affirmation undergoes a basic change. Thus speaking of the same particularity Jaspers can also affirm:

> The truth which Existenz acquires here in coming to itself is purely phenomenal, but the phenomenon as such, objectively conceived and held fast, is not the truth; it was true only because there was transcendence in it at the same time.[22]

And again, speaking specifically in terms of the truth of ciphers, he can observe:

> Previously the cipher contents themselves were the final authority; now a higher one must decide whether or not truth speaks through the ciphers at a certain moment, within certain limits. The higher authority lies...in the living practice of Existenz.[23]

Truth, in other words, is decided not by what the particular contents mediate but by how they occasion the immediacy of Existenz.[24]

Now the point of this review of Jaspers' notion of ciphers--and of the resulting clarification of the priority of function over content in his understanding of existential truth--is to show that Jaspers does indeed undercut the strong sense of particularity which he must sustain in order to make good on his intended resolution to the problem of pluralism and truth. For in terms of the two senses of particularity distinguished above, Jaspers clearly does establish the necessity of historic particularity as a vehicle or occasion for the attainment of truth. Truth is attainable, in his language, only via the adoption of particular belief contents as ciphers. But the transformation of those particular contents which is a condition of their adoption, and thus a condition of their possible truth, negates that other sense of particularity whereby the particular contents as such mediate transcendent truth. For as we have seen, it is not by virtue of their contents but by virtue of their function (which is to bring those contents into suspension) that ciphers are true. In terms of particular contents, then, ciphers remain irreducibly plural and opposed. Or, to put the matter more exactly, those irreducible oppositions whence the problem of pluralism and truth arose in the first place remain insofar as different beliefs are understood in terms of their particular contents. In terms of their truth, however, or when those same beliefs are understood in terms of their function as ciphers, the opposition of contents is no longer a matter of significance. Rather they all serve *in the same way* as vehicles for transcending faith by virtue of the fact that their particular (opposed) contents "are stripped of objective reality." If they were not thus "stripped of objective reality" and consequently of their mutual opposition--if, for instance, the Christian doctrine of biblical revelation were still to be understood to mean that God in fact does speak in an absolutely unique way in the literature of this particular book--then they would not have been appropriated as ciphers and would not be true.

Jaspers would, of course, reject this whole line of argument on the grounds that content and function cannot thus be separated but are precisely what is held together in the process of adoption. I think it is nearer the truth, however, to suggest that Jaspers' discussion of pluralism and truth derives much of its seeming plausibility by playing upon the ambiguity involved in different ideas of truth and different senses of particularity (and thus of plurality). A possible plurality of true religions can be affirmed in terms of Jaspers' understanding of truth. Yet the character of that plurality has been changed or reduced from the plurality of particular and opposed beliefs (which were deeply problematic in terms of the question of the truth of their contents) to a plurality of particular but only accidentally different vehicles (which can be equally true in terms of the truth of their function).

For all of the inevitability of particular and different beliefs to "mediate immediacy," then, a significant plurality of the type envisioned in proposed resolutions to the pluralism and truth dilemma is finally not possible on Jaspers' terms. Thus his account of the logic of religious truth fails to sustain the possible plurality it intends to affirm. Truth resides essentially in the movement of Existenz, in that inwardness or immediacy for which any particular mediator is simply a necessary, but in terms of its particular content finally indifferent occasion. It is, rather, Existenz which is the sole real mediator, all other mediators being true only insofar as they occasion or serve as means for this single mediator. Rather than speak of Jaspers' affirmation of a plurality of true religions, then, it would be more accurate to speak of his affirmation of the one true (philosophical) faith in terms of which all other (religious or philosophical) faiths must be transformed if they are to be true. Thus there is finally room in Jaspers' thought for the affirmation of particularity in the strong sense of that term--for that one particular set of beliefs or, more broadly, that one particular vision of humanity which Jaspers regards as finally and thus normatively true (in the quite ordinary and straightforward sense of that term).[25] His philosophy affirms, in other words, that one significant particularity which Heinrich Barth refers to as the 19th Century idealist vision of human autonomy with its essentially inner and unfettered relation to the divine.[26] In terms of the question of religious (or philosophical) pluralism, that vision is singular insofar as it does not exclude other historic particulars as different and opposed, but includes or absorbs them by transforming all oppositions and appropriating all particularities as so many different springboards for the one movement of inner transcending. Thus it does provide a framework for religious plurality, but at the price that all real difference is embraced and nullified in the name of an overarching unity to history--a unity found in the immediacy of the autonomous subject.[27]

The answer to the specific question which has been the focus of discussion in this dissertation, then, is negative. The logic of religious truth proposed by Jaspers does not in the end provide a basis for the view that a significant plurality of religions could all strictly speaking be said to be true. Yet as has been clear from the beginning, Jaspers' efforts have not simply been directed to the resolution of a logical puzzle. They have, rather, been an attempt to find an adequate account of religious truth--an account which would be adequate not only for a situation of pluralism but above all for a situation of crisis. Thus before turning to some brief and concluding suggestions concerning the fundamental reasons for the failure of Jaspers' effort, it would be valuable, I think, to examine in a bit more detail the character and extent of that failure.[28] If, in other words, Jaspers fails to provide a logic for a plurality of true religions because of his failure to sustain a strong sense of particularity, what is the more general significance of this loss of particularity for the adequacy of his account of religious truth? Does his thought still provide an adequate way of understanding religious plurality and truth even if it does not provide a basis for affirming a significant plurality of true religions? Or is the actual (as distinct from the intended) result of his thought inadequate not only as an account of religious plurality but also as an account of religious truth? Does it, in effect, far from establishing the intended possibility of a plurality of true religions, actually constitute a negation not only of plurality but also of religion?[29]

As noted on more than one occasion in the preceding pages, Jaspers insists on the eminently positive character of religious faith as that which distinguishes it from philosophical faith, on the one hand, and from the ersatz syntheses of supposedly universal religions, on the other. Yet it is, once again, just this positive element of the particular religions which would seem to be negated or transformed in their appropriation as ciphers. Jaspers, of course, would distinguish between that "embodiment" which must be negated and the religious positivity which remains even when religious particularities are transformed as ciphers.[30] Yet it is far from clear exactly what real difference this distinction is supposed to convey. For if the idea of the positive character of religious faith implies certain specific types of relations (such as reverence and worship) to certain particularities which are taken as "the actuality of something specifically holy in places, objects, and acts,"[31] then it is difficult to see how such relations can remain when they are subsumed within that controlling type of relationship dictated by Jaspers' notion of cipher--a relationship characterized by the continual negation or bringing-into-suspension of particular contents ("stripped of objective reality"[32]). If, in other words, the sense of particularity which is actually affirmed by Jaspers' thought is not sufficient to allow a significant plurality of religions, then how can it be sufficient to sustain the strongly positive particularity which by Jaspers' own reckoning is essential for any specifically religious truth?

Once again the issue here is a complex one since, as noted, not only the descriptive theory but also the actual usage of the different religions bear testimony to various ways of balancing mediation and immediacy, or of holding together affirmation and negation in an appreciation of the sacramental. There are constant traditions within the great religions, such as the *via negativa* within Christianity to which Jaspers often refers,[33] which seem to emphasize transcendence to the exclusion of any positive qualification or mediation of the divine. Similarly there are those who would argue that true religion must constantly be released from its "Babylonian captivity," purified of all positivity, and understood as essentially a matter of inwardness or as a purely vertical transcending (via whatever inevitable symbols) to the total otherness of the divine. Standing against such an understanding of religion as pure inwardness, however, is the historical reality of the central significance of certain particular mediations (origins, scriptures, doctrinal formulations) in all of the world's great religions. Against the tendency to purify faith of all particular contents stands the argument that faith without contents (in traditional Western terms, *fides qua* without *fides quae*) is self-destructive, like "casting an anchor in shifting sands."[34] Far from purifying and liberating faith such a purification actually destroys the pathos of faith, rendering it directionless and apathetic, and contributing further to the present crisis "in which our alternatives seem increasingly to be reality divested of symbols or symbols divested of reality."[35] On balance, then, Jaspers would seem to be essentially correct in asserting that it is the presence of positive mediations which is the distinguishing characteristic of religion.[36] On balance, too, however, it would seem to be just such positivity which his understanding of the logic of religious truth effectively undercuts.

Jaspers' philosophy is, as he admits, "religious" in a very general sense of that term.[37] Thus it does in fact provide a basis for that type of non-dogmatic religiousness which is today quite widespread. As the German philosopher Johannes Thyssen notes:

> In an age which has largely lost its belief in the Christian dogmas, and which in its uncertainty and anxiety looks out for a new "hold," such a hold in divine Being is offered here....In this sense Jaspers practices a far-reaching "demythologizing" and he says with regard to myths and revelations that his philosophy tries to retain their contents, though their claim to validity cannot stand. This endeavor, the sincerity and difficulty of which we have witnessed, is in fact an appeal to all who seek a spiritual hold and have access to philosophy. It leads the way to undogmatic religion by means of philosophy (in some respects comparable to the young Schleiermacher).[38]

Such "undogmatic religion" is, however, as Jaspers is quick to point out,[39] something quite different from the specific particularity of religion properly so called. Just how great that difference is has been well described by C. S. Lewis in the account of his own conversion. (I will cite at length because of the relevance of Lewis' description to Jaspers' discussion of religion.) Speaking of that philosophical idealism which first provided him with a "spiritual hold," Lewis notes:

> ...this proved that our discursive thought moved only on the level of "Appearance," and "Reality" must be somewhere else. And where else but, of course, in the Absolute? There, not here, was the "full splendor" behind "the sensuous curtain." The emotion that went with all this was certainly religious. But this was a religion that cost

> nothing. We could talk religiously about the Absolute; but there was no danger of Its doing anything about us. It was "there"; safely and immovably "there." It would never come "here," never (to be blunt) make a nuisance of Itself. This quasi-religion was all a one-way street; all *eros*...steaming up, but no *agape* darting down. There was noting to fear; better still, nothing to obey.[40]

This general religion might, of course, as in Lewis' own case, serve as a preparation for a more specifically religious conversion.[41] Or it might, as seems often the case today, serve for those so inclined or so situated by reason of personal history as a way of remembering and reappropriating the specifically religious faith of their tradition even after they have ceased to believe in the truth of the particular contents of that faith. (In reality, of course, it is actually the specifically religious contents which in such cases "serve" as a vehicle for that general undogmatic faith.) But it is at very least highly questionable whether even such remembering and reappropriating can long sustain itself. Traditions are, after all, remembered and reappropriated because they are believed to be true--because, in the terms used above, their contents are believed to be true. Unless the truth of a tradition in this sense is the basis of commitment to it, and not commitment the basis of its truth, the tradition has already died. Put somewhat differently, "once we know that horizons are relative and man-made, their power to sustain us is blighted. Once we know them to be relative, they no longer horizon us. We cannot live in a horizon when we know it to be one."[42]

Jaspers, for instance, in one of the few cases where he makes specific recommendations about the future reappropriation of particular religions, speaks continually of "biblical religion" and of the necessity for the West to retain that specific biblical heritage which has been one of its most profound origins.[43] Yet as Ronald Gregor Smith remarks, it is hard to understand how the biblical tradition which Jaspers regards as so crucial can survive without Jews, Christians, and Muslims--without, in other words, communities of those who take specific contents of biblical faith to be true.[44] To be sure, Jaspers would maintain that this is precisely what Jews,

Christians, and Muslims must do if they are to attain truth. Yet in so doing, in taking "specific contents of biblical faith to be true," they must simultaneously keep those contents suspended as ciphers. In what sense then, to reiterate the basic question upon which this entire critique of Jaspers has been focused, are the *contents* of biblical faith "taken to be true"? Or, to put the matter somewhat differently, why would Jews, Christians, and Muslims want to return continually to the difficult adoptive struggle with these particular contents when those contents can be true only as ciphers (or functionally)? What basis is there in the logic outlined by Jaspers for such a narrowing of focus or, more generally, for any narrowly religious relationship to specific, positive particularities? Has not the sole solid basis for such specifically religious wrestling (i.e., belief in the truth of particular contents and positivities, however difficult or dialectical its attainment) been undermined? It would seem that Jaspers' thought in actual effect provides, rather, a basis for that loosening and eventual loss of particularity whereby contemporary religious man would become "like a Don Juan courting all the gods."[45] Or even where the effect of Jaspers' thinking is not so extreme, even where the particular contents of traditional belief might still be "taken up as true," they would, I think, be worn far too lightly when taken up as true in Jaspers' sense of the word.

Thus the problematic character of Jaspers' thought concerning religious truth runs rather deep. It is not just that his thinking does not provide a basis for the reappropriation of particular religious faiths in their diversity, nor even that it provides no solid footing for the remembrance of such remnants of the religious faiths which have thus far survived the present crisis. Rather by negating the strong sense of particularity and positivity which are fundamental to both plurality and religion it actually contributes to that decline of religious faith which it hopes to combat. (Here, once again, is the fact of actual contradiction between intention and performance.) In the image suggested by one of Jaspers' most sympathetic critics, his thinking stands like a Trojan horse within those very traditions he hopes to preserve.[46] While proclaiming the desirability and possibility of present reappropriation of the various religions in their diversity, it undercuts the basis of that diversity and of the possible truth of each particular tradition, and absorbs the different traditions into the unacknowledged unity of a prior or more fundamental (and non-religious) faith. Jaspers' thought, moreover, effects this negation even as it depends for its own truthfulness upon the continuation of those traditions which it negates--thus sawing off, so to speak, the branch it is sitting on.[47] And this undercutting of his own position is true in an even more general sense insofar as his thought in effect negates that particularity which by its own account is crucial to the logic of existential truth. At best, then, Jaspers' philosophy makes possible the truth of an undogmatic religious faith which transforms the traditional religions into so many of its own accidentally different vehicles. At worst, however, it unintentionally cuts the ground out from any possible affirmation of religious truth, simultaneously throwing itself and any notion of transcendent faith into serious question.

3.

By way of conclusion I would like briefly to suggest an explanation for Jaspers' failure to provide an adequate account of religious truth, an explanation which, I believe, points in a more fruitful direction for thought about the question of pluralism and truth. What follows, however, cannot be understood as a necessary conclusion from the preceding critical arguments, nor is it essential to the completion of those arguments. Still, since it does flow from that argumentation, it is presented here as a concluding note--a postscript which at this point remains quite literally (and not ironically) "unscientific," or an afterthought which sketches ideas that need to be taken up in more critical detail in later work.

Throughout the present work, in both the presentation of Jaspers' thought and the subsequent critique, the issue most central to the discussion of pluralism and truth has been the issue of particularity. Any attempt to argue for the possibility of a plurality of true religions and, more generally, any attempt to provide an adequate account of religious truth must, I have maintained, allow sufficient weight or status to the particularity characteristic of religious truth--to the particular contents or claims whereby the various traditions stand distinct and in opposition, and to the particular positivity characteristic of religion as such. Jaspers is aware of this requirement and the affirmation of such particularity is clearly central to the logic whereby he intends to resolve the dilemma of pluralism and truth. Yet that intention, as we have seen, is contradicted when the significance of his affirmation of particularity is changed by other aspects of his thought which are in tension with or, more accurately, antagonistic to it. In the preceding pages the effect of this basic antagonism in Jaspers' thought has been described in terms of the specific character of the dialectic involved in his understanding of religious truth and then in terms of the way in which that dialectic changes or transforms the type of particularity which is actually affirmed or sustained.

In all of the preceding critique, however, there has not yet been any real explanation of this fundamental antagonism. Why is it, in other words, that performance undercuts intention? What is it in Jaspers' thought that brings about the effective loss of that emphasis upon particularity which it needs to maintain? The answer, I want to suggest, is to be found not in some detail of his explicit defense of particularity (Chapter IV) but in the framework (Chapter III) within which that defense occurs. Said somewhat differently, the basic tension or antagonism in his thought can best be understood as a tension between the intentions and affirmation of his defense of particularity, on the one hand, and the foundations upon which that defense is built, on the other. Jaspers provides what is probably the best account of particularity (or certainly one of the best) that is possible within the framework provided by those foundations. The inadequacy of his account, then, suggests a more basic inadequacy in those foundations. (Thus the remark repeated frequently above that a full critique of Jaspers' discussion of religious truth would take us to today's most fundamental and controversial issues.) It suggests, in other words, that there is something about those foundations which is inimical to the type of emphasis upon particularity required for an adequate account of religious plurality and truth. It further suggests, then, that the effort to find a more adequate account would have to build upon different foundations or to move in fundamentally different directions.[48]

Of course the foundational or fundamental framework within which Jaspers develops his defense of particularity is what has here been continually referred to (in summary fashion) as his essentially Kantian understanding of subjectivity and objectivity, knowledge and freedom. It is, to put the matter in a slightly different way, the shared heritage of 19th Century German idealism to which Jaspers gives a current and particularly Kantian expression. These foundations, then, represent and express an extremely complex and sophisticated tradition of human thought. Yet for all their complexity they fail to provide the basis for an adequate account of religious particularity and they pervert that affirmation of such particularity which Jaspers' thought intends. Thus while I can do so only with very broad strokes and at the price of great oversimplification, I want to suggest why these foundations are essentially problematic for thought about religious pluralism and truth.

The image of a "Copernican revolution" was, of course, used by Kant himself to indicate the fundamentally (or foundationally) new point of departure for his thoughts. It proclaimed a fundamental inversion of the priority of subject and object as the focus of thought. And it is, I believe, this inversion--or perhaps it would be more accurate to say it is the particular Kantian understanding of subject and object and of their relations in knowledge and freedom--which is at the root of the failure of Jaspers' discussion of religious pluralism. For Jaspers, as we have seen, lays the foundations for that discussion by analyzing the dichotomy of subject and object. Yet the emphasis and weight of this analysis falls heavily upon the subject, and not simply on the subject as the center of consciousness, but above all on the subject as active and free. The basic and controlling program of Jaspers' thinking is from the first, then, the Kantian denial of knowledge to make room for freedom and then to understand faith in terms of that freedom.

Thus while the various elements in Jaspers' "system" are interwoven in a fluid and changing way, it seems clear that the real center of his thinking is the idea of freedom given with the understanding of subjectivity as Existenz. This idea of freedom, moreover, while quite widespread, is also a quite particular, even peculiar understanding of freedom and subjectivity. On its terms, a human being is fully human, or becomes a person, only insofar as she or he becomes an autonomous self. And becoming an autonomous self, or becoming subjective, means being free in such a way that there are, at least in that personal realm where freedom is possible, no obstacles, no "other" which stands over against me and lays claim upon me thereby negating my autonomy. To put the matter differently, knowledge and freedom are, as we have seen throughout in Jaspers' thinking, basically incompatible. Where there is knowledge (or revelation) and the constraint of facts and objects, there can be no freedom. Freedom arises only at the limits of knowledge, or on the boundary, where objectivity and the definite are kept suspended by the dialectical movement of thought. What arises at the boundary for Jaspers is not the absolute and absurd freedom of that existentialism against which much of his thinking is directed. Nor is this boundary and the emergence of Existenz, as we have seen, somehow totally separable from existence, from the world of objects and events and knowledge. Yet freedom can emerge (and thus faith can become possible) only with the dialectical suspension of such objects and events and knowledge. The controlling image in Jaspers' thinking, then, is that of a certain type of freedom or autonomy, a certain type of authentic human subjectivity, which is finally possible only via the exclusion or subordination of otherness.

Thus the understanding of subjectivity which is central to the foundations of Jaspers' thought entails a corresponding sense of objectivity. Historically, of course, the emergence of the understanding of freedom which is foundational for Jaspers' thought was, as already suggested, integrally connected with the loss of the traditional idea of nature (as *telos*) and the rise of modern science. It is, in other words, inseparable from a severe limitation not only of the scope but also of the meaning of knowledge and objectivity. In the Kantian language employed by Jaspers, only phenomena, objects as they appear to us, are knowable, and then only in always restricted horizons or frames of reference. Such objects, moreover, are not directly relevant to our basic human or existential questions. More generally, then, the world as such contains no word for us as human beings, no answer to our fundamental human questions. It is, to play upon Jaspers' metaphor, only at the boundary and never at the center of things that such an answer might be found. Or, in another of his telling metaphors, even if it is possible to experience that boundary only in the realm of existence, or only through the world of objects and events, that answer is experienced as a *breakthrough* which shatters the actuality of the objective. It would appear, then, although much more would have to be said in order to make this account adequate, that the definite otherness which we encounter in various ways (whether as physical objects, or ideas, or persons, or events) must inevitably play a limited and, I think it is fair to say, *merely* functional role which corresponds to the understanding of freedom in Jaspers' scheme of things.[49] Frequently an obstacle, it can at best serve as a means or a mediator, but never in such a way that it hinders the more fundamental priority of freedom or immediacy.

Thus the "Copernican revolution" of Kantian thought results in that specific understanding of subjectivity and objectivity which is foundational for Jaspers' discussion of religious truth and which is, finally, the basic reason for the inadequacy of that discussion. For within the framework established by this fundamental understanding of subjectivity and objectivity it does not seem possible to maintain the significance of those definite mediations which are, even on Jaspers' own terms, an essential aspect of religious truth and a fundamental condition of significant religious pluralism.

If, then, discussion of religious pluralism and truth is to be something more than (self) deception veiling the gradual disappearance of all diversity, if in other words it intends (with Jaspers) to take plurality and thus particularity seriously, then it would seem that such discussion must (against Jaspers) take place within more adequate foundations. It must attempt to reassemble the pieces of the puzzle within a framework fundamentally different from Jaspers', within an understanding of subjectivity and objectivity which would allow a far more positive appreciation of objectivity and thus a more complex picture of subjectivity. It must, for instance, be based upon an understanding of objectivity which could admit the possibility of a word spoken in answer to the fundamental human questions not (or not only) at the boundary, but at the center of things, through particular (and thus possibly plural) mediations. And it must be based on an understanding of subjectivity which could better accommodate those typically religious attitudes of reverence, worship, and obedience which arise in response to such particular mediations. In more general terms, then, a potentially adequate approach to the question of religious pluralism, and more specifically to the quest for an understanding of religious truth which could admit the possibility of a plurality of true religions, must be based in some way upon a basic change in the direction of thinking, a reversal, so to speak, of the previous (Kantian) inversion of the priority of subject and object.

Having said this, of course, one has in a sense said very little. For while there are discussions of religious pluralism and truth which seem to move in the direction indicated by this conclusion,[50] it is at best only a general direction. The simple assertion, moreover, that such a general change in direction is necessary begs the really difficult question of whether it is possible--whether, in other words, a more adequate understanding of subjectivity and objectivity can be established and what such an understanding would look like. Still, if Jaspers is correct in claiming that the foundations of his thought articulate pervasive conditions governing life and thought in our age--and I think he is basically correct in this claim--then perhaps the rather minimal suggestion that one cannot think fruitfully about the question of religious pluralism within his foundations is not altogether insignificant. If, in other words, the preceding critique of Jaspers is fundamentally correct, then the analysis of Jaspers' thinking (and thereby of a predominant type of contemporary thinking) will at least have succeeded in calling into question a major and temptingly available avenue for thought about the problem of religious pluralism--even if it leaves the hard questions unanswered and the hard work yet to be done. That hard work would involve a far more fundamental critique of Jaspers' thought than was attempted here as one step toward the establishment of a more adequate foundational thinking. It would involve a more positive effort to think through the problem of religious pluralism and truth in terms of this changed direction and these more adequate foundations. For the present, however, it must suffice to suggest that those are the tasks of the future.

INTRODUCTION

NOTES

[1]While the concern of this entire study is to move toward a more adequate understanding of what is meant by "religious truth," a few preliminary remarks about the way in which the term is being used here are called for. In the first place, religious truth refers to the truth claimed by a religion or the truth *of* religion as distinct from various historical or sociological or descriptive truths *about* religion. Thus, secondly, the term is used here in the quite straightforward sense that religions--even when, as is often asserted, for instance, about forms of Buddhism, they make no claim to deal with speculative theological or metaphysical issues--make claims about "the way things really are" at least insofar as the reality of human destiny and salvation are concerned. Religious truth, then, refers primarily to the truth claims or proposals for belief made by a particular religion. Cf. William A. Christian, *Meaning and Truth In Religion* (Princeton, NJ: Princeton University Press, 1964), pp. 4-6, 10-14. Finally, this primary sense of the term involves the corresponding claim made by the religions to provide a true way or ways of living in accord with the proposed truth of belief.

[2]This characterization of our age as well as this entire introductory discussion of the problem is obviously, for purposes of brevity, sketched with very broad strokes.

[3]Karl Rahner, *Inquiries*, 1964. Cited by James Schall, "The Nonexistence of Christian Political Philosophy," *Worldview*, 19 #4 (April 1976), pp. 29-30.

[4]Cf. *New Essays In Philosophical Theology*, eds. Anthony Flew and Alasdair MacIntyre (London: SCM, 1968), pp. 96-130.

[5]Cf. especially the work of scientist-philosopher Michael Polanyi and discussions inspired by his thought.

[6]John Hick, *Philosophy of Religion* (2nd ed.; Englewood Cliffs, New Jersey: Prentice-Hall, 1973), p. 119.

[7]While a record or survey of the recent rise in such actual encounter has yet to be attempted, two significant examples from among many for North American Christians would be the person, life and death of Thomas Merton--cf. for example, his collection *Mystics and Zen Masters* (New York: Dell, 1967)--and the 1972 Mount Savior "Symposium on World Spiritualities" recorded in *Word out of Silence*, the special double issue of *Cross Currents*, XXIV #2-3 (Summer-Fall 1974), 133-395.

[8]An attempted complete listing even of very recent literature would be vast indeed. Works which have been used in this study are listed in a special section of the Bibliography.

[9] *Philosophy of Religion*, p. 119.

[10] What follows is simply a brief evocation of the problem which makes no claim to completeness. An analysis of Jaspers' understanding of the problem is presented in the next chapter. For a good, still brief, but more detailed discussion of the factors leading to this new sensitivity to religious pluralism, cf. Charles Davis, *Christ and the World Religions* (London: Hodder and Stoughton, 1970), pp. 26-39.

[11] This is, evidently, not to suggest a relativist equation of religion and culture, but only to state the obvious fact that "any concrete formulation of a religion...has to integrate it with a culture." John Dunne, *The Way of All the Earth* (New York: Macmillan, 1972), p. 126. For a detailed argument about the necessary interweaving of religion with culture, cf. Wilfred Cantwell Smith, *The Meaning and End of Religion* (New York: New American Library, Mentor Books, 1964).

[12] It is perhaps worth noting in passing that it is a failure to take seriously this first, critical aspect of the present situation which gives to many discussions of the second aspect, the convergence of the religions, such an air of unreality. The rhetoric of pluralism rings hollow when it ignores or hides this pervading homogeneity.

[13] Wilfred Cantwell Smith, "Comparative Religion: Whither--and Why?", in *The History of Religions*, eds. Mircea Eliade and Joseph Kitagawa (Chicago: The University of Chicago Press, 1959), p. 32. The "Symposium on World Spiritualities" referred to above, n. 7, clearly illustrates this change as also does the framework of even such academic studies as Ninian Smart's *World Religions: A Dialogue* (Baltimore: Penguin, 1969) and William Christian's *Oppositions of Religious Doctrines* (London: Macmillan, 1972), Chapter II.

[14] One way of formulating the "theological" issue faced by any particular faith would be: given the truth of that religion as normative, although not necessarily exhaustive or exclusive, in what sense might other religions also be considered true? For a good discussion in the shift in theological questions resulting from the new situation, cf. Davis, pp. 39-48.

[15] It is necessary to be clear that no claim is being made here about the relative significance of these different questions or about their truth (insofar as one question either presupposes or precludes the answer to another). It is simply claimed that for many persons today consciousness of religious pluralism comes to focus in the last-mentioned question and the purpose of this study, then, is to try to shed some light on the legitimacy of this way of thinking about pluralism and truth. It may well be that this "modern consciousness" which precludes the possibility of any one religion being the truth, far from being the key to an adequate understanding of the problem of pluralism and truth, is itself the basic problem. To borrow a phrase from Wittgenstein, it may be a picture which holds us captive and bewitches our intelligence. Cf. John Kane, "Pluralism, Truth, and the Study of Religion," *Studies in Religion/Sciences*

Religiouses IV #3 (1974/75), pp. 158-168, for a development of this suggestion. Cf. also Davis, pp. 26-39 for a discussion of the clear bias and intolerance in the widespread, yet *a priori* rejection of the very possibility that any one religion could be universally or normatively true--a bias which is at least implicitly reinforced by the noncommittal character of religious studies in the secular university.

[16]John Hick, *God and the Universe of Faiths* (London: Macmillan, 1973), pp. 120-132.

[17]*Ibid.*, p. 103.

[18]J. G. Arapura, *Religion As Anxiety and Tranquility* (The Hague/Paris: Mouton, 1972), p. 3.

[19]*Ibid.*, p. 4.

[20]Christian, *Oppositions of Religious Doctrines*, p. 116.

[21]Smart, p. 12.

[22]Christian, *Oppositions of Religious Doctrines*, p. 5.

[23]The geographic metaphor is suggested by Peter Munz, *Problems of Religious Knowledge* (London: SCM, 1959), p. 8.

[24]The real problem with theories of general or essential religion is not so much that they are a sort of intellectual imperialism with reductionistic consequences, but that in seeking to be comprehensive they become empty and ephemeral.

[25]Maurice Friedmann, "Touchstones of Reality" in M. Friedmann, T. Patrick Burke, and Samuel Laeuchli, *Searching in the Syntax of Things: Experiments in the Study of Religion* (Philadelphia: Fortress Press, 1972), p. 23.

[26]Schleiermacher himself, as a Christian theologian, argued the normative priority of the Christian faith. Yet in escaping the Enlightenment dilemma of *either* natural *or* positive religion he developed an essentially Kantian understanding of a religious *a priori* which at once rejected natural or general religiousness and affirmed the inevitability and validity of different, particular, historic religions as expressions of that *in se* inexpressible *a priori*. It is this type of analysis which has become influential and the basis for the view that more than one religion can be true. For a somewhat fuller discussion of Schleiermacher in this context, and a brief comparison of Schleiermacher and Jaspers, cf. Kane, esp. pp. 160-161.

[27]How often, for instance, one hears the idea that different religions are concretely irreducible, yet both (all) true because transcendentally unified.

[28]Owen Thomas, ed., "Introduction" to *Attitudes Toward Other Religions* (New York: Harper & Row, 1969), pp. 20-21.

[29]There is, of course, a way of understanding the claim that more than one religion is true which does not incur this logical difficulty. George Burch, for instance, in his *Alternative Goals in Religion* (Montreal: McGill-Queen's University Press, 1972), argues that the major religions are equally true because they each proclaim radically different, exclusive but not contradictory, truths--three separate, complementary absolutes. This interesting, if highly speculative, view is not the type of position under consideration here.

[30]Cf. William Christian's discussion of the limited role of such "critical philosophy" in *Oppositions of Religious Doctrines*, pp. 8-12.

[31]Cf. Chapter II for Jaspers' analysis of the world-historic significance of this issue--an analysis in which both Kierkegaard and Nietzsche are figures of prominent importance.

[32]The German original was published in 1962 and the English translation, *Philosophical Faith and Revelation*, in 1967. (As already noted, bibliographic data about reference to Jaspers' major works is found in the general Bibliography below.) While there has been considerable discussion of the work in Europe, it has taken place almost entirely within theological circles in response to Jaspers' call for the transformation of Christian self-understanding. Although such discussion is clearly relevant to the issue of religious pluralism, there has been no major discussion of the problem of pluralism as such. In the "Introduction" to his recent book *Karl Jaspers: Philosophy as Faith* (Amherst: University of Massachusetts Press, 1975), p. 11, Leonard Ehrlich announces a planned volume which will deal with the question of pluralism, i.e. with "Jaspers' effort to promote truth in religion by means of a philosophical critique of religion" at least "insofar as it pertains to that volume's topic of the political import of Jaspers' philosophical concern."

[33]No significant thinker is reducible to a type, just as no type, however well conceived, is adequate for what it is intended to include. It is such difficulty with the notion of "types of thinking"--above all the way in which types can so easily, even unintentionally, become "strawmen" fitted to the purposes of one's argument--which has led to the present focus upon the actual work of one thinker.

[34]Cf. above all the 1956 "Epilogue" to Jaspers' 1937 lectures originally published under the title *Existenzphilosophie* (PE, pp. 95-96) as well as the 1955 "Epilogue" to the third edition of his *Philosophie* (Ph I, pp. 11-12). What Jaspers rejects is not only the catch-word which "remains like a phantom under whose name the most heterogeneous things are treated as identical" (PE, p. 96), but specifically existentialism as an attempt to absolutize human freedom (Sartre) and as an attempt to develop an ontology of freedom (Heidegger).

[35]Only his famous debate with Bultmann on "the question of demythologizing" (published in English as *Myth and Christianity*) is widely known, and that primarily because of theological interest in Bultmann.

[36]Heinrich Fries, *Ist der Glaube ein Verrat am Menschen? Eine Begegnung mit Karl Jaspers* (Speyer: Pilger-Verlag, 1950), p. 20.

[37]PA, pp. 76, 78; PSP, pp. 95-103, 112.

[38]Ph I, pp. 296-316; cf. PA, p. 77. For a survey of Jaspers' discussion of religion in his earliest writings, prior to *Philosophie*, cf. T. J. von Lutz's *Reichweite und Grenzen von Karl Jaspers' Stellungnahme zu Religion und Offenbarung* (Dissertation: University of Munich, 1968), pp. 1-45.

[39]Ehrlich, p. 11.

[40]*Philosophical Faith and Revelation* is, of course, the basic text in this regard, but it is the culmination of a long development of thinking about the logic of faith (in *Philosophy* and *Von der Wahrheit*) and about the crisis of the present age (especially *The Origin and Goal of History*). While explicit discussions of religion are to be found in these major works as well as in numerous articles or chapters of shorter works, the most readily available summary statements of Jaspers' thought about religion prior to *Philosophical Faith and Revelation* are *Der philosophische Glaube* (1948, English trans. *The Perennial Scope of Philosophy*, especially Chapter 4), *Die Frage der Entmythologizierung* (1954, English trans. *Myth and Christianity*), and the sections on religion in Jaspers' "Philosophical Autobiography" (pp. 75-81) and his "Reply to My Critics" (pp. 777-785) in P. A. Schilpp, ed., *The Philosophy of Karl Jaspers* (New York: Tudor, 1957). N.B., this last mentioned work will hereafter be referred to simply as "Schilpp."

[41]This is one of the central arguments of Lutz's dissertation. (Cf. n. 38 above.)

[42]Ph I, p. 301.

[43]PA, pp. 65-69, 81-84; OMP, pp. 135-136.

[44]PFR, p. 88.

[45]OGH, pp. 225-227; cf. pp. 214-215, 221-225.

[46]Ph I, p. 296; PA, p. 77; R, pp. 779, 755-756.

[47]Cf., for example, Robert Bellah's essays "Transcendence in Contemporary Piety" and "Between Religion and Social Science" in *Beyond Belief: Essays on Religion in a Post-Traditional World* (New York: Harper & Row, 1970), pp. 196-208, 237-259.

[48]VdW, p. 192. While the claim might seem arrogant on any terms, Jaspers is not claiming some "Hegelian" synthesis of all of Western thought. He rejects the possibility of such a synthesis. His claim, rather, is to be able to provide, at this juncture in Western history ("standing on the shoulders of giants"), a critical or methodological framework for the rich and profound diversity of Western thought--one which hopes also to be significant for the emerging world horizon of thought. Cf. PA, pp. 70-75, 81-84.

[49]RE, p. 153, n. 1.

[50]Ehrlich, p. 210, recounts a conversation with one of the current professors of philosophy at Basel who referred to Jaspers as "the first and last Kantian."

[51]Karl Löwith, *Nature, History, and Existentialism* (Evanston: Northwestern University Press, 1966), p. 31.

[52]These themes are exlicitly developed in Jaspers' 1935 lectures published as *Vernunft und Existenz* (English trans. *Reason and Existenz*). Cf. especially lectures one and five. Cf. also Chapter II of the present study.

[53]OGH, pp. 226-227.

[54]Ph I, p. 251. Emphasis added.

[55]E.g., PSP, pp. 89-96; PFR, p. 342.

[56]PSP, p. 113. Cf. PW, p. 150; OGH, p. 221.

[57]PSP, pp. 90-91.

[58]Jaspers himself, agreeing with a critic, notes that "in a certain sense" his philosophy "does not *have* a philosophy of religion," but "*is* itself philosophy of religion." R, p. 778.

[59]The confluence of concern about religion, politics, and a global "philosophical logic" developed gradually for Jaspers. Cf. the accounting in his own autobiography, PA, pp. 53-81, and the excellent account in Hans Saner's brief biography *Karl Jaspers* (Reinbek bei Hamburg: Rowohlt, 1970), pp. 82-113.

[60]Ehrlich, p. 10.

[61]PFR, p. 13. The whole of *Philosophical Faith and Revelation* is intended as part of a dialogue or, to use Jaspers' term, a "loving struggle" with the representatives of more orthodox religious self-understanding.

[62]While it is true that *Philosophical Faith and Revelation* is the one work where Jaspers recapitulates the essence of his thinking about religious pluralism, that work itself runs to some three hundred and sixty closely printed pages (almost five hundred and fifty in the original German text) *and* it cannot be read without reference to the original texts of *Philosophy* (three volumes, nine hundred pages) and *Von der Wahrheit* (one thousand fifty pages) from which its basic thinking is drawn. In addition there are at least twelve shorter books (as well as various essays) parts of which bear directly on the discussion of religion, and, given the systematic, interconnected character of Jaspers' thinking, an almost unlimited number of discussions throughout the entire corpus which bear at least indirectly on the topic of religious truth and pluralism.

[63]Ph I, pp. 33-34; II, pp. 100-103.

[64]E. B. Ashton, "Translator's Note" to *Philosophy*, Vol. I, pp. xiv.

[65]Letter to Jean Wahl dated Nov. 8, 1949, cited in Jean Wahl, *La Pensée de l'Existence* (Paris: Flammarion, 1951), pp. 286-287, n. 1.

[66]Cf. PFR, pp. 112-115. Jaspers speaks of "building by tearing down what we have built." Ph I, p. xv.

[67]The metaphor is from Xavier Tilliette, *Karl Jaspers: Théorie de la Vérité; Metaphysique des Chiffres; Foi Philosophique* (Paris: Aubier, 1960), p. 7. Ehrlich (p. 1) suggests a more mechanical metaphor: "We meet more or less recurring methods and methodologies, concerns and conceptions, distinctions and syntheses which, functioning as sources of disquiet much in the manner of horologic balances, move and direct the structure." One is also reminded at times of Wittgenstein's famous metaphor about "criss-crossing in every direction" over a wide field of thought in the course of his philosophical journeyings. Cf. *Philosophical Investigations* (Oxford: Basil Blackwell, 1963), p. vii.

[68]VdW, pp. 911-912; OMP, pp. 157-158. Jaspers criticizes what he recognizes to be one of the best interpretations of his thought, the work of Dufrenne and Ricoeur, for being "too clear," for "reducing his work to a rigid framework." Cf. Jaspers' "Preface" to M. Dufrenne and P. Ricoeur, *Karl Jaspers et la Philosophie de l'Existence* (Paris: Editions du Seuil, 1947), p. 7. Cf. also the remark attributed to Jaspers in Sebastian Samay, *Reason Revisited: The Philosophy of Karl Jaspers* (Dublin: Gill and Macmillan, 1971), p. 257.

[69]PA, p. 39. What Jaspers says here regarding the individual chapters of *Philosophy* is equally true for all of his books.

[70]As if to frustrate the desire for such a summary, Jaspers has himself, especially on the occasion of public lectures, given several "summaries" of his thinking, each different from the others and each involving the stylistic characteristics just noted. Cf. *Philosophy of Existence* (1937 lectures); *The Perennial Scope of Philosophy* (1947 lectures); *Way to Wisdom* (1950 lectures); and *Philosophy is for Everyman* (1964 lectures).

[71]Ph I, p. 18. Cf. I, p. 34: "If anything has been accomplished in this *Philosophy* it is not an expoundable doctrine, but a movement of thought,...a movement to be entered into if one is to understand its meaning."

[72]Ph I, p. 16.

[73]PA, p. 70.

[74]Ehrlich (p. 22) refers to Jaspers' style as "invocatory" thinking while Tilliette (p. 41) speaks of "*la methode incantatoire de Jaspers*."

[75]Cf. Bernard Welte, *La Foi Philosophique chez Jaspers et Saint Thomas d'Aquin* (Desclee de Brouwer, 1958), pp. 19-20, 16-17.

[76]James Collins, "Jaspers on Science and Philosophy" in Schilpp, p. 115.

[77]Such interpretation inevitably involves a transformation of the original into one's own thinking and the risk that what results is more interpretation than Jaspers. The risk is unavoidable. Cf. Welte, p. 16.

CHAPTER II

NOTES

[1]OGH, p. 61.

[2]There are two major writings, *Die geistige Situation der Zeit* (1931, English trans. *Man in the Modern Age*) and *Vom Ursprung und Ziel der Geschichte* (1949, English trans. *The Origin and Goal of History*), along with various essays and sections in other works.

[3]Tilliette, p. 61.

[4]Hannah Arendt, "Karl Jaspers: Citizen of the World" in Schilpp, p. 541. Emphasis added.

[5]Cf., for example, the opening paragraphs of his massive theoretical work *Von der Wahrheit*, pp. 1-2.

[6]PA, p. 70.

[7]Ph I, pp. 43-45.

[8]WW, p. 108. Jaspers argues this point at length and with detailed reference to the present situation of the West in *Reason and Existenz*, especially Chapter I ("The Origin of the Contemporary Philosophical Situation") and Chapter V ("Possibilities for Contemporary Philosophizing").

[9]Ph I, pp. 11-12. Cf. RE, p. 152, n. 1.

[10]WW, p. 108. Emphasis added. Here is the full meaning of the point made in the preceding chapter that Jaspers' thought seeks to be typical of our age "in the best sense."

[11]As the formulations cited above indicate, this mediation consists of an endlessly dialectical movement between the extremes, and not in some supposed ("Hegelian") synthesis. The latter, as Hegel knew, would only be possible at the end of history--an end which Jaspers clearly does not claim. RE, p. 48.

[12]RE, pp. 135-137. Jaspers' understanding of the historicity of thought and truth will be developed in detail in Chapter IV, yet even in the present brief discussion there is a clear indication of the way in which Jaspers thinks within modern historical consciousness in recognizing relativity (and thus plurality) while still affirming truth. The extremes which he rejects, on the other hand, would, each in its own way, dissolve the problem of plurality and truth--the historicist claim by recognizing plurality but negating truth, the metaphysical claim by affirming one truth and denying plurality.

[13]EH, pp. 35-36.

[14]The two published volumes on *The Great Philosophers* as well as individual studies and numerous articles on other thinkers are only a part of a projected, but never completed, "world history of philosophy" which was to encompass the thought of both East and West and to contribute, thereby, to the foundations of the coming era of global history. Cf. Hans Saner's report, "Zu Karl Jaspers Nachlass" in Saner, ed., *Karl Jaspers in Der Discussion* (Munich: R. Piper and Co. Verlag, 1973), pp. 455-459, on the scope and complexity of this project which occupied Jaspers for about twenty-five years and which covers more than twenty-two thousand pages (!) of notes and manuscripts in his literary estate.

[15]Cf. OGH, p. 233.

[16]Golo Mann, "Freedom and the Social Sciences" in Schilpp, p. 559.

[17]EH, p. 61.

[18]Mann, p. 557.

[19]For Jaspers' strictures against such total knowledge, strictures which apply equally to his own analysis, cf. MMA, pp. 26-30 and OGH, pp. 267-268.

[20]What follows is not an attempt to touch on all aspects of Jaspers' analysis of the present age, but to elucidate the center of that analysis particularly as it bears upon the question of religious truth and pluralism.

[21]OGH, pp. 81, 97; MMA, pp. 22-23; PFR, p. 29.

[22]OGH, p. 24.

[23]OGH, pp. 125, 98.

[24]OGH, pp. 96-97.

[25]OGH, pp. 98-99. Cf. pp. 111, 122-123; PFR, p. 314.

[26]EH, p. 66.

[27]OGH, pp. 127-134, 266.

[28]PE, p. 4.

[29]OGH, p. 139. Cf. pp. 193-213.

[30]Arendt, p. 540.

[31]PFR, pp. 30-32.

[32]OGH, p. 138. Cf. OMP, p. 138.

[33]OGH, pp. 141-228, esp. pp. 214-219; PFR, pp. 286-320. This is the theme of the already-cited and incisive article by Hannah Arendt (in Schilpp, pp. 539-549). Cf. also Jürgen Habermas, "Die Gestalten Der Wahrheit" in Saner, ed., *Karl Jaspers in der Discussion*, pp. 309-316.

[34]OGH, *passim*; cf. esp. pp. 22-26, 71-77; and WW, pp. 96-104.

[35]EH, p. 35.

[36]Cf. OGH, pp. xiii-xvi, 267-268.

[37]It also illustrates in a particularly forceful way the extent to which Jaspers himself shares in that critical/historical (his critics would say historicist) consciousness which is so pivotal or crucial to the inner core of the crisis.

[38]OGH, p. 1.

[39]OGH, p. 1.

[40]It will be evident that Jaspers' conception of a universal axis contains already in germ the whole of his thinking on religious pluralism. It is a tribute to the power (or seductiveness?) of his vision that it has become commonplace in much contemporary thought and particularly in thought about the question of religious pluralism. Cf., for instance, Hick, *God and the Universe of Faiths*, pp. 134 ss. and Dunne, pp. 136-137.

[41]OGH, p. 1.

[42]OGH, p. 25.

[43]This is not to say that those who lived before, or who live outside the scope of this breakthrough in the three spheres are somehow excluded from truth. For Jaspers the substance and truth of human existence can be attained and lived in the most diverse forms, however "primitive" (prior to or outside the axis of history) or "secular" (subsequent to a loss of the axial heritage). It is to say, however, that the awareness and expression given to that substance in the "three great cultural spheres" during the Axial Period has in fact been decisive for the course of human history and is crucial for the present situation.

[44]The idea that insight or truth is touched in situations of crisis, at the limits or boundaries when all securities have fallen away, is central to Jaspers' understanding of existential truth. Cf. OGH, p. 243.

[45]OGH, p. 2. By a similar, yet more telescopic delineation of the Axial Period (one which includes the origin of the Christian era as the extension of Jewish prophecy) Jaspers points to those "paradigmatic individuals" who emerged to express what is basic and ultimate in human existence and who stand, each uniquely different, at the very heart of their

respective traditions: Socrates, Buddha, Confucius, and Jesus. Cf. GP:F, Part I.

[46]As John Hicks notes, it is above all at the level of "differences in the key or revelatory experiences that unify a stream of religious experience or thought" that "the largest difficulty in the way of religious agreement" is found. *Philosophy of Religion*, pp. 127-128.

[47]Cf. OGH, pp. 2-6, 54-57.

[48]The tantalizing vagueness or ambiguity of this discussion of the content of the axial breakthrough is Jaspers' own and it is, as noted above, deliberate. On the one hand the very idea of a single axis, and continual use of words like "breakthrough," "lucid awareness," and "faith" all suggest an ascertainable common content. Yet this Jaspers denies even though he is aware that talk of an "inexpressible unity" is logically contradictory. On the other hand he clearly wants to suggest something far more profound than a merely formal similarity of certain accidentally simultaneous transitions in major world cultures. Such would not constitute an axis for world history and a common basis for future communication. The difficulty here, of course, is the central difficulty in the question of religious pluralism and truth.

[49]It was already noted, but deserves reiteration, that the two "turning points" are not parallel. The present is no new Axial Period. It seems, rather, almost a reversal of the Axial Period. Its rough parallel is the hypothetical Promethean Age and thus it admits the possibility of a future or second Axial Period (just as it admits the possibility of a total night of nihilism or some transformed reappropriation of the first axial heritage). OGH, p. 25.

[50]OGH, pp. 57, 59, 62-66, 74-75, 88-93.

[51]GP:O, p. 250; OGH, p. 75.

[52]Clearly for Jaspers the rise of modern science and technology is that which "brought about the tremendous crisis." Yet he resists speaking of it as "*the* cause" because "the origin of the crisis cannot be apprehended in a single cause" but "in the infinite web of material and spiritual interconnections of historical change," and because the origins of modern science and technology (themselves closely connected, yet distinct and causally related) are also multiple, complex, and finally enigmatic. Cf. OGH, pp. 135, 103-105, 88-93. Thus while science and technology are more immediate causes of the present crisis, "the spiritual movements that led up to ourselves began long before the world was altered by technology." OGH, pp. 135-136.

[53]MMA, pp. 4-15.

[54]On Jaspers' analysis of the significance of Kierkegaard and Nietzsche for our era, cf. RE, Chapter I and the articles "The Importance of Kierkegaard" and "The Importance of Nietzsche,

Marx, and Kierkegaard in the History of Philosophy." For Jaspers' view on the way in which two wars have rudely awakened us to their truth, cf. his short treatise *The European Spirit.*

[55]The image and interpretation, while my own, are suggested by Jaspers: OGH, pp. 139-140; PSP, p. 159.

[56]OGH, p. 77. Emphasis added.

[57]To say this, however, is not to replace a materialist theory of causality with an idealist one. Jaspers, as already noted, follows his mentor Max Weber in rejecting all monocausal explanation in history. Cf. MMA, pp. 15-17.

[58]As noted above, "the spiritual movements that led up to ourselves began long before the world was altered by technology." OGH, pp. 135-136.

[59]The phrase suggests the typical sense of a turning *to* man, but also, and consequently, a turning or change *in* man.

[60]At one point Jaspers speaks of "the two streams" of modern thought which determine our present situation, one which flows from the natural sciences and a second which is constituted by modern (critical) philosophy. Cf. "The Importance of Nietzsche, Marx, and Kierkegaard in the History of Philosophy," p. 229. Jaspers, as scientist and philosopher, claims to draw from both streams. It is clear, however, that his own understanding of the new conditions governing life and thought are a distillation of that critical shift in thinking which has been effected at least since Descartes and above all by Kant. Nietzsche and Kierkegaard, as noted, awaken us to what has actually happened in that thinking.

[61]Of course all of the exposition of Jaspers' thought in succeeding chapters, and especially in the next chapter, is "further elucidation" of this shift in consciousness.

[62]PFR, p. 50. Cf. pp. 50-60.

[63]PFR, p. 51.

[64]PFR, pp. 288-292.

[65]Jaspers' discussion of the present, interestingly enough, does not so much stress as presuppose the absolute centrality of the idea of freedom at the core of the contemporary crisis. This is perhaps because freedom is so fundamental to *all* of his thinking. On freedom and the crisis cf. OGH, pp. 152 ss. and PFR, pp. 292-297. On the centrality of the idea of the autonomous self in Jaspers' thought and its roots in German Idealism cf. the very important article by Heinrich Barth, "Karl Jaspers über Glaube und Geschichte," in *Karl Jaspers in der Discussion*, pp. 275-277.

[66]This sense of freedom is well expressed in Lessing's famous aphorism that man's worth is found not "in the truth he possesses" but "in everlasting striving after truth."

[67]Here again Jaspers does not so much stress as presuppose the centrality of the modern idea of history in the crisis of contemporary consciousness. And again this is probably because his own thinking is so deliberately conditioned by that change. Jaspers' understanding of the historicity of thought has already been touched on at the beginning of this chapter and will be taken up in detail in Chapter IV.

[68]The "inner" shift in consciousness could also be characterized, in terms of man's relation to nature, as a separation or even alienation from nature given with the modern understanding of reason, freedom, and history. It is illustrative of the shift and of Jaspers' thinking within it that a discussion of nature is not fundamental to his thought in the way the anthropocentric themes of reason, freedom, and history are.

[69]OGH, pp. 214-219, 266; PSP, pp. 172-176.

[70]PA, pp. 83-84. Cf. Saner, *Karl Jaspers*, pp. 104-105.

[71]In the obituary which he composed for himself he speaks of this work as a ceaseless effort to find a way "from the end of European philosophy into an approaching world-philosophy." "Nekrolog von Karl Jaspers selbst verfasst," *Gedankenfeier für Karl Jaspers am 4 März 1969 in der Martinskirche*, Basler Universitatsreden 60 Heft (Basel: Verlag Helbing und Lichtenhahn, 1969), p. 41.

[72]PFR, pp. 294-295.

[73]PSP, pp. 174-176.

[74]EH, p. 61.

[75]PSP, p. 159.

[76]The assertion that "there is no other way" must be clarified. The future may well see an absolute break where only a new Axial Period, a new "revelation" of some sort would rekindle the light of faith. The future is open and it will not be determined by human action alone. It is finally a matter of grace and destiny. Still "it is probable that the faith of the future will continue to move within the fundamental positions and categories of the Axial Period." OGH, p. 225. In any event, *our* attitude cannot be one of fatal passivity. It must (paradoxically) be a response to the challenge of our fate. And for Jaspers this means that the responsible path in the struggle for humanity (for faith) is that dialectic of recourse to the past within the present. Cf. OGH, pp. 226-228.

[77]OGH, p. 131.

[78]MMA, p. 152. Cf. OGH, p. 132.

[79]Cf. OGH, pp. 132-134, 216-219; PSP, pp. 118-146, 159-164.

[80]While most of Jaspers' concrete examples of such fixation are taken from Western Christianity, it is clear from what he says generally about the present age that he sees this process as a world-wide possibility. There are, moreover, scattered references to the process of fixation in the other religions, particularly in Confucian China: cf. VdW, p. 811; GP:F, pp. 71-72. Still, both because his own situation and immediate concern is Western Christianity, and because the claim to exclusive possession of the truth attained a unique form in the Christian doctrine of revelation, Jaspers focuses his discussion primarily on the crisis of Western religion.

[81]Such "catholicism" is found not only in the Catholic Church, but "everywhere in the world." VdW, p. 833 n. 1. Cf. Jaspers' entire discussion of the decay of true authority into fixed untruth: VdW, pp. 789, 819-830, and 832-868 (esp. 833, 835, 841-842, 847-50).

[82]Cf. PFR, pp. 44-48. Yet the basic content of traditional faith "will always offset the totalitarian trend" so that such "catholicism" remains worlds apart from the horrors of modern (secular) totalitarian rule. PFR, p. 47.

[83]MMA, p. 178.

[84]PFR, p. 322.

[85]Of course the *distinction* between philosophy and religion has a complex history, but the possibility of their *separation*, as two independent realms of faith, is distinctively modern. Cf. PFR, pp. 52-55. Such philosophical faith, however, is no rarefied phenomenon restricted to an academically trained elite. It is independent faith found wherever free and thoughtful self-realization characterizes individual existence.

[86]PSP, p. 112.

[87]PFR, p. 320.

[88]PFR, p. 320.

[89]Of course the new situation could also give rise to a universal faith. Not, of course, the empty abstractions of some syncretist or universal religion. We have already seen that Jaspers dismisses such "cosmopolitanism." The only world faith which is actually possible is that ideological pseudo-faith which would accompany the rise of a totalitarian world-state--a possibility to be dreaded, not desired.

[90]PSP, p. 109.

[91]PFR, p. 41. Cf. pp. 329-346.

[92]PSP, pp. 108-109; PFR, pp. 322 ss. Jaspers, as already noted, claims that philosophy and religion have separated in the modern West so that one in fact walks the path of either religious or philosophical faith. The accuracy of this claim can be questioned and, more significantly, the extent to which

Jaspers himself respects this separation can be questioned. As will be seen, one of the fundamental criticisms of his understanding of religion concerns whether the transformation of religion he calls for is not, in fact, a transformation of (a plurality of) concrete religious faiths into (a single) philosophical faith.

[93]PFR, p. 342. Cf. PSP, pp. 88-97; VdW, pp. 816 ss., 833 ss; OGH, pp. 226-227. This is a call *not* for the renunciation of particular traditions and their claims, but of the universal validity which those claims have always entailed. Arendt, p. 541.

[94]VdW, p. 817. Of course for Jaspers it is this very reference *to transcendence* which necessitates the renunciation of exclusivity for all immanent forms.

[95]As noted, Jaspers focuses primarily on "biblical religion" both because it is the religion with which the West must be concerned and because only in the sphere of "biblical religion" with its particular understanding of revelation has the claim to exclusivity become a central and explicit doctrine of immense consequence. PSP, p. 92. Cf. PSP, pp. 88-97 and PFR, *passim*.

[96]PFR, p. vii.

[97]PFR, p. viii.

[98]Cf., for example, the various criticisms summarized in Werner Schneiders, *Karl Jaspers in der Kritik* (Bonn: H. Bouvier and Co. Verlag, 1965), pp. 116-123, 226-228.

[99]H. Barth, p. 279.

[100]Thus Jaspers' thought would indeed "stand unmistakably under the aegis of Hegel." *Ibid*, p. 281. Cf. pp. 276-279. A concrete plurality of religions would be subsumed (*aufgehoben*) into the unity of philosophical faith.

[101]Cf. RE, pp. 37-39 on Kierkegaard and Nietzsche as "exceptions" and Walter Kaufmann's "Jaspers' Relation to Nietzsche" in Schilpp, pp. 407-436, for an extreme example of such a critique of this use of Kierkegaard and Nietzsche.

[102]Thus the distinction made in the previous chapter between Jaspers' own faith and his analysis of the logic of faith would disappear.

[103]Cf. Chapter I, p. 18 (above).

[104]GP:O, p. 250. Cf. p. 116: "The realities confronting him were not what he believed them to be, and he was essentially unaware of this fact and its consequences."

[105]PFR, p. 88.

CHAPTER III

NOTES

[1]Jaspers' term, "*ein Grundgedanke*," admits of both translations: a thought, as in a set of ideas, or a process of thinking. It will be clear to anyone familiar with Jaspers' writings that the idea of "foundational thinking" discussed in this chapter is broader in scope than Jaspers' literal use of the term "*Grundgedanke*." The reason for this is discussed below.

[2]VdW, p. 24.

[3]Gabriel Marcel, *Creative Fidelity*, trans. Robert Rosthal (New York: Farrar, Strauss and Co., 1964), p. 222.

[4]VdW, p. 871.

[5]Consistent with his "great care to avoid too much terminological precision," Jaspers speaks equally of a *Grundgedanke* (singular: foundational thought or thinking), of *Grundgedanken* (plural: foundational ideas), of a *philosophische Grundewissen* (a "basic philosophical knowledge" which, however, he explicitly contrasts with knowledge in the ordinary sense of "cogent, generally valid cognition," cf. PFR, p. 89) or more generally of a *Denken der Ursprunge* (thinking of or to origins) and a *Philosophie des Umgreifenden* (philosophy of the encompassing). Cf. VdW, pp. 24, 28, 29, 42, 44, 190.

[6]*Das Umgreifende*, the "encompassing" (or the "comprehensive" as it is sometimes translated) is the term developed by Jaspers to designate the never graspable presence of being as the source or origin of that which appears according to various irreducible modes within the subject-object dichotomy of experience. Cf. below pp. 65-67.

[7]At one point Jaspers notes that he had at various times made four different attempts at a "systematic outline" of his thought. Cf. OMP, p. 158. Even more significant are the numerous instance of "typical sequences of foundational thinking" from various angles or points of departure both within each of the major works and throughout the shorter writings. Cf., for example, VdW, pp. 29-46, 871-902; Ph I, pp. 43-90; Ph II, pp. 3-32; OMP, pp. 138-155; PSP, pp. 1-23; PE, pp. 3-29.

[8]Saner, *Karl Jaspers*, p. iii. Much, of course, needs to be said about the complex of various internal interrelations between these two massive works. Cf., for instance, the important article by Ernst Mayer, "Philosophie und philosophische Logik bei Jaspers," in Saner, ed., *Karl Jaspers in der Discussion*, pp. 224-232. It must suffice here to compare their remarkable unity, yet irreducible difference, to two musical

compositions by the same master--written years apart, with different frameworks, yet employing most of the same themes and somehow achieving the same effect. As Tilliette says (pp. 21-22), "they interpenetrate without repeating each other, and mutually presuppose each other....there is perhaps a difference of inflection, a displacement of accent, but certainly no rupture, nor even properly speaking an evolution."

[9]PFR, p. 87.

[10]Ph I, p. 18.

[11]VdW, p. 28.

[12]Ph I, p. 34.

[13]The absolutely central concepts of "transcendence" and "encompassing," for example, designate not objects, but directions of thinking.

[14]R, p. 802; PFR, pp. 82-83, 88-89.

[15]PSP, pp. 29-30. For consistency of usage throughout the present work, the translation of *Umgreifende* here (and elsewhere) has been changed from "comprehensive" to "encompassing."

[16]*Op. cit.*, p. 33.

[17]As will be seen below, the idea of transcending is at once, inseparably, "transcendental" (or critically self-conscious of the conditions of thought) and "transcendent" (in moving beyond the limits of knowledge). Key texts descriptive of this transcending are to be found in Ph I, pp. 76-89; Ph III, pp. 30-39; VdW, pp. 35-42; PFR, pp. 74-82.

[18]RE, p. 75. Cf. Ph I, pp. 1, 34.

[19]PFR, pp. 76-78.

[20]PFR, p. 4; cf. CT, pp. 12-13.

[21]Ph I, p. 44 (from the opening lines of Jaspers' *Philosophy*).

[22]Thus Jaspers' preference in his writings on history for those periods and persons caught in critical change since they are moments of disillusioned clarity about the fundamental human situation. The paradigm for all such moments is, of course, the Axial Period.

[23]PFR, pp. 4-5; CT, pp. 12 ss.

[24]VdW, pp. 703, 871-874; Ph I, pp. 47-48.

[25]Marcel, p. 250. It is worth noting that while Jaspers' further analysis of this basic situation is presented in less dark, more abstract terms such as "fundamental limitations," "basic antimonies," and "the subject-object dichotomy," the

basic experience seems one of almost unrelieved alienation. Thus the world is in constant and "irresistable" flux (Ph I, pp. 43-44); it is "dark," "disjointed," "depleted and entangled" (Ph I, p. 59); ever phenomenal or objective, it seems a "prison" which shackles freedom (PFR, pp. 77, 79). This darkness is seen again, later, in the centrality to Jaspers' thinking of the boundary situations of death, suffering, struggle, guilt and more generally of "the dubiousness and historicity of all existence" (Ph II, pp. 193-222). Thus while there are clear parallels between this evocation of the human situation and "the great traditions of religion and thought," there may well be other significant parallels with the heretical traditions of gnostic thought. Cf., for instance, Hans Jonas' essay "Gnosticism, Existentialism and Nihilism," in *The Gnostic Religion* (2nd ed.; Boston: Beacon Press, 1970), pp. 320-340, which does not refer directly to Jaspers, but contains suggestions not irrelevant for understanding Jaspers.

[26]PFR, p. 4. Jaspers cites Augustine's testimony to the depth of such questioning: "I am cast into the world...I have become a question unto myself...." PFR, p. 5.

[27]OMP, pp. 139, 142-152. Jean Wahl notes how the three volume structure of *Philosophy* corresponds to Kant's basic questioning about world, soul, and God. *La Pensée de l'Existence*, p. 78.

[28]PE, p. 14.

[29]VdW, p. 35; cf. pp. 871-902.

[30]Samay, p. 4. This, as Samay notes, is the thesis of Gabriel Marcel's previously cited interpretative essay on Jaspers' thought.

[31]Jaspers' term "Existenz" will hopefully be clarified in subsequent discussing of the foundational thinking. It stands in contrast to *Dasein*, which Jaspers uses to mean "empirical (human) existence"--getting and spending, knowing and doing. Consistent with the practice of Jaspers' translators, it is here left untranslated, just as Jaspers himself did not attempt a translation into German when he took the term from Kiekegaard's Danish.

[32]PFR, pp. 5-6. Cf. VdW, pp. 356, 965.

[33]*Op. cit.*, p. 232.

[34]"The question is: What is being? The question to this question is: how can I and how must I think of being?" VdW, p. 37.

[35]PE, pp. 16-17.

[36]Ph I, p. 45.

[37]As noted above, pp. 35-36, nn. 67 and 68, Jaspers himself does not so much focus on, as presuppose this shift in the understanding of world from "world as nature" to "world as

history." Karl Löwith notes that the one thing which unites the various philosophies grouped together as "existentialism" is the "modern destiny" that "the physical universe...is present only as the insignificant background of man's forlorn existence" and "the negative experience that man has no definite place and nature within the natural universe." The world for such thinking is "*our* world...a world without nature." Löwith, *Nature, History, and Existentialism*, pp. 103-104.

[38]PFR, p. 50.

[39]Cf. Ph I, pp. 120-225; RAR, pp. 7-37; OGH, pp. 81-95; and the article "Philosophy and Science" in WW, pp. 147-167. On Jaspers' understanding of science, cf. James Collins, "Jaspers on Science and Philosophy" in Schilpp, pp. 115-140, and Samay, pp. 71-135.

[40]PFR, p. 51.

[41]Collins, p. 118. Cf. pp. 125-126: "the scientific interest is to secure the maximum clarity, logical necessity, universality, and communicability in its determinate object. Scientific inquiry is guided by the ideal of rational objectivity, guaranteed by evidence that is universally valid and compelling in a universal way."

[42]Ph I, pp. 123-127, 163-164. Cf. Samay, pp. 89-92.

[43]"I acquire cogent insight, but the cogency does not become absolute." Ph I, p. 122; cf. pp. 123-126.

[44]Jaspers traces those aberrations of science which claim the possibility (or the actual possession) of a completed system of total knowledge (*Totalwissen*) to that fascination with modern science which entered the realm of properly philosophic thinking above all through the influence of Descartes. Today, despite the significance of the sciences, accurate understanding of the nature of science is "exceedingly rare" while the various pseudo-scientific forms of supposed total knowledge are a pervasive danger. OGH, pp. 93-96; cf. RAR, *passim*.

[45]PFR, p. 31. OGH, p. 87: Science is "the real investigation of questions that are always determinate and particular."

[46]OGH, pp. 83-87. Cf. Ph I, pp. 127-135.

[47]VdW, p. 97.

[48]PFR, p. 7; CT, p. 8. Thus the ground or source whence things appear is not itself knowable. We know beings, but not being. "To our cognition 'Being in itself' is a boundary concept, not an object." PFR, p. 7. It is important to note that at this point Jaspers moves from a description of scientific knowing to a philosophical (Kantian) interpretation of the nature of knowledge.

[49]VdW, p. 96. Cf. OGH, p. 94.

[50]VdW, pp. 96 ss.

[51]CT, p. 7. While Jaspers can speak of "the real, rich, glorious, and terrible world" (PFR, p. 7), in fact the world as knowable is finally the same fragmented endlessness which provoked fundamental questions. It is reminiscent of Pascal's dark evocation of human life cast adrift in the infinities of space and time. Cf. Löwith, *Nature, History, and Existentialism*, p. 103.

[52]PFR, p. 7.

[53]*New Essays in Philosophical Theology*, p. 96.

[54]PFR, p. 51.

[55]CT, pp. 8-9. Cf. Ph I, pp. 77-78.

[56]OGH, pp. 83-85.

[57]Ph III, p. 6; cf. Ph II, pp. 173-174.

[58]Peter Wust early characterized Jaspers' philosophy as an "*entscheidungs Irrationalismus*" in *Ungewissheit und Wagnis* (München: J. Kösel Verlag, 4 ed., 1946), pp. 273-284 (originally published in 1937).

[59]For Jaspers freedom is not arbitrariness or blind risk or "an imagined possession of absolute freedom." Rather "the substance of freedom is a pursuit of illumination." PFR, p. 6. Put somewhat differently, "reason and Existenz are not two opposed powers...Each exists only through the other. They mutually develop one another and find through one another clarity and reality." RE, p. 68.

[60]"The truth that makes itself felt at the boundary of science is infinitely more than scientific correctness." OMP, p. 148.

[61]With Kant, Jaspers finds the world, the self, and God all "beyond the limits of knowledge." The self which can become an object of knowledge, of psychological knowledge for instance, is not the never objectifiable depth of the self. That depth is experienced, becomes present and thus is brought to awareness (*innewerden*), only as ever historic action, as the exercise of freedom. "I do not know what I am in the original transcending to myself, but I come to the sense *that* 'I am.'" Ph I, p. 85; cf. Ph II, pp. 26-42.

[62]Ph II, p. 3.

[63]It is, in Jaspers' suggestive alliteration, "*Durchbruck, nicht Dauer*." VdW, p. 454; cf. pp. 710 ss.

[64]Ph I, p. 77.

[65]Ph I, pp. 78, 80, 81.

[66]Ph I, p. 78.

[67]Ph I, p. 82.

[68]Dufrenne and Ricoeur, p. 51.

[69]Welte, p. 46.

[70]Cf. Ph II, pp. 178-222. There are clearly many differing elucidations of Existenz and transcendence throughout the second and third volumes of *Philosophy* and throughout *Von der Wahrheit*. The discussion of boundary situations is selected here as illustrative, not exhaustive, because it is an aspect of Jaspers' thinking which has become rather widespread in contemporary thought.

[71]Ph II, p. 178 .

[72]Ph II, p. 181. The need for and significance of this shift in perspective cannot, of course, be demonstrated to one who has not already experienced such a conversion.

[73]Ph II, pp. 188, 192.

[74]For Jaspers' elucidation of these particular boundary situations, cf. Ph II, pp. 193-218.

[75]Ph II, p. 218.

[76]Ph II, pp. 218-221.

[77]WW, pp. 21-22.

[78]Ph II, p. 178: "*There is no way to survey them in existence*, no way to see behind them." To know a boundary would already be to stand outside or beyond it, in which case it would not be an absolute boundary.

[79]VdW, p. 880.

[80]Cf., for instance, his more detailed elucidation of the "original motion" leading to this decisive point in Ph II, pp. 228-240. It would seem, moreover, that this decisive point might well arrive and be met in a brief pause, an utterly simple act, the quiet recall of assent or resolve in the midst of daily life and attention to very ordinary, little things.

[81]Ph III, p. 5.

[82]Ph III, p. 5.

[83]Yet Jaspers' understanding of suicide is not simplistic. Cf. Ph II, pp. 262-273.

[84]VdW, p. 881. Jaspers' understanding of Buddhism, for instance, is very similar to those who find its assertion of

absolute emptiness (*śūnya*) an affirmation of absolute transcendence. Cf. PFR, pp. 265-268; GP:O, pp. 416-433 (on Nagarjuna) and T. R. V. Murti, *The Central Philosophy of Buddhism* (London: George Allen and Unwin, 1960).

[85]Ph III, pp. 6-7; cf. PE, pp. 25-26.

[86]Jaspers' elucidation of absolute consciousness follows and completes that of boundary situations. Cf. Ph II, pp. 223-254. Absolute consciousness is not "consciousness of an object," nor is it "experience as an object of psychology." It is, rather, "something that I experience actively in my own self-ascertainment as fulfilled freedom, but I never have it before me as what it is." It is "not the being of Existenz, but its self-assurance" because "it is for Existenz the assurance of being." Ph II, pp. 223-225.

[87]Ph II, p. 243. Cf. PSP, p. 17: "Faith...is the existential act by which transcendence becomes conscious in its actuality."

[88]Reference to faith typically abounds throughout Jaspers' writings. For explicit discussions of faith, cf. especially Ph I, pp. 255-262; Ph II, pp. 243-246; OGH, pp. 215-228; and above all PSP (German title *Der philosophische Glaube*), pp. 1-46. In the already cited book by Leonard Ehrlich, *Karl Jaspers: Philosophy As Faith*, faith is, with much justice, taken as the central notion for interpreting Jaspers' thought.

[89]Jaspers continually struggles against mysticism, whether as wordless union "out of this world" or as (consequent?) vision received "in this world." Cf. PFR, pp. 264, 279-281; Ph II, pp. 182, 244, 277 ss.; Ph III, 169 ss. Ehrlich, pp. 40-56.

[90]Jaspers sides with Kierkegaard in the latter's critique of this notion in both Schleiermacher and Hegel. While he would surely grant the presence of a vital (animal?) confidence as a condition for knowing and doing, faith is neither generalized nor necessary, but always historic and free. Cf. PSP, pp. 9-10.

[91]Ph II, pp. 243, 245.

[92]What Jaspers says of philosophy as one form of faith is true more generally of faith as such: "Philosophy does not live by reason alone, but it can take no step without it" (RE, p. 131). The inseparability of reason and Existenz is the central theme of the lectures by that title (*Reason and Existenz*). Cf., especially, pp. 67-68.

[93]Cf. PSP, pp. 42-45.

[94]Ph III, p. 4. Clearly the answer of faith is not a permanent possession, but neither is it an absurd glorification of merely endless searching as in Lessing's parable where man chooses "the ever-active search for truth" (even on condition of endless failure) rather than "pure truth" which belongs to

God alone. Jaspers' position seeks a *via media* between these extremes. Thus Tilliette (p. 60) errs in equating Jaspers and Lessing.

[95]Ph II, p. 247. Generally, however, despite his avoidance of fixed terminology, he reserves the term "revelation" to a religious, even exclusively Christian context. Cf. OGH, p. 226; PFR, pp. 8-10, 15-37.

[96]Ph II, p. 106. "*Dasein*" is the German word which Jaspers here and elsewhere uses, in contrast to "Existenz," for referring to concrete, this-worldly human "existence."

[97]Ph II, p. 244.

[98]Ph II, pp. 244, 246-247. Faith is inseparable from "contents of faith." It is always "faith in something." Cf. PSP, pp. 8, 24-46.

[99]Jaspers' essential protestantism is articulated in his continual return to "the rule of transcendence: 'Thou shalt not make unto thee any false image or likeness.'" PFR, p. 136; cf. PSP, p. 80.

[100]PSP, pp. 9, 11.

[101]VdW, pp. 29-222. Cf. PFR, pp. 61-91; PSP, pp. 11-19; RE, pp. 51-76; PE, pp. 15-29; and WW, pp. 28-38. The "basic philosophical knowledge" developed in these first sections of the philosophical logic, especially the central ideas sketched here, are Jaspers' *Grundgedanke* in the narrower sense--the logical groundwork of framework of his own *Philosophie*, the framework within which he hoped diverse faiths might meet in this age of crisis. The full significance of the framework, however, is found only in the details of the foundational thinking sketched above which it recapitulates and without which it would seem, one fears, a mere *tour de force*.

[102]PFR, pp. 7, 61. Jaspers' word is "*Spaltung*," which literally means "cleavage" or "split" and thus carries the implication of original unity. For convenience, I have followed the general practice of Jaspers' translations in using the word "dichotomy" which retains somewhat the implication of estrangement that might be lost entirely in speaking only of a "polarity."

[103]PFR, p. 61.

[104]PSP, p. 28. Jaspers does not use the term "horizon" since any horizon is a limited or relative whole. The encompassing, rather, is that "further behind the horizon which is continually manifest where there is an horizon" and which "encloses every attained horizon without itself being a horizon." VdW, p. 38.

[105]PFR, p. 61.

[106]Cf. PFR, p. 69; VdW, pp. 26, 158-159.

[107]PSP, pp. 30-31. The whole discussion here quite evidently presupposes an awakening to basic questions and critical clarification whereby the subject-object dichotomy is experienced as a basic, indeed an absolute boundary.

[108]VdW, pp. 37-42; PFR, pp. 76-79; PSP, pp. 17-19.

[109]PSP, p. 17.

[110]PGO, p. 132 (=PFR, p. 77).

[111]PSP, p. 18.

[112]PFR, p. 78.

[113]PFR, p. 61.

[114]PFR, p. 69.

[115]It is not ontology, but "periechontology"--Jaspers' coinage for thought about the encompassing (Gk., *periechon*). Cf. VdW, pp. 158-161; PFR, p. 75.

[116]PFR, p. 69: "We must feel each mode, yield to it, awaken to it."

[117]Cf. VdW, pp. 45-113; PFR, pp. 61-69. What is summarized here is evidently just an empty list without the suggestive detail of these original texts.

[118]Ph I, p. 85. Cf. OMP, p. 140: "The meaning of *truth* assumes another value."

[119]PE, p. 36 (my translation of *Bewusstsein überhaupt*).

[120]OMP, p. 148.

[121]Cf. RE, p. 77: "In each of these modes being and truth have a distinct sense." RE, p. 80: "Truth is not of one sort, single and unique in its meaning. It has as many senses as there are modes of communication in which it arises. For what truth is is determined by the character of the encompassing within which communication takes place."

[122]Cf. VdW, pp. 601-653 for details and PE, pp. 33-41 for a summary presentation.

[123]PE, p. 41. Cf. VdW, pp. 654-709 and PE, pp. 41-61 for fuller discussion of the interrelation of the various types of truth and the quest for the unity of the one truth.

[124]VdW, p. 839. Cf. PFR, p. 83. Jean Wahl calls this the great "antimony" of unity and plurality in Jaspers' understanding of truth. *La Pensée de l'Existence*, pp. 103 ss.

[125]It could probably be argued that discussion of the four types of truth and their interrelations, however interesting in itself, serves primarily to safeguard against the

reductionistic consequences usually involved in a bifurcation of truth into cognitive and existential truths. Jaspers' entire life's work may with justice be understood as a continual struggle against precisely such pervasive reduction whereby the most important truth becomes merely an affair of the heart (in contrast to the head) or a matter of private values (in contrast to hard facts). Whether the content of his thought enables him to succeed in this intention is, of course, the central critical question about his philosophy.

[126] PW, p. 150.

[127] Jean Wahl, *La Pensée de l'Existence*, p. 96. For Jaspers, as for Kant, the incompatibility of knowledge and freedom is a central premise of ethics and of religion. Ethics is possible only where freedom is not determined by nature, and religion is possible only where God has not "enslaved" man by the direct revelation of his presence. Jaspers, of course, also draws upon Kierkegaard's reflections on this incompatibility. Cf. Jean Wahl, "Notes on Some Relations of Jaspers to Kierkegaard and Heidegger," in Schilpp, pp. 393-400.

[128] Note Jaspers' paradoxical formula: "The truth...before all truth and more than all truth is the divinity." VdW, p. 461.

[129] PW, p. 150. Jaspers' position here can be contrasted with an understanding of "existential truth" in terms of which the incompatibility of the truth of knowledge and existential truth is only provisional, not final. On this view, freedom or subjectivity is seen as the sole way to the ascertainment of transcendent truth. Certain things can be known only in certain ways, but they can be *known*. Thus what is understood and affirmed existentially is not historic. It is finally and objectively and thus universally true. Jaspers might well respond to this suggestion with an image from Kierkegaard: the dancer, superb when he leaps, is farcical when he attempts to fly, and tragic, too, since he soon forgets how to leap.

[130] Cf. Ph I, p. 296 ss; PSP, p. 78 ss; R, p. 779.

[131] Ph III, p. 107. Cf. PSP, p. 113.

[132] Jaspers has no illusions that his call for this transformation will be met with great enthusiasm by orthodox believers. The entire polemic of *Philosophical Faith and Revelation* is aimed at orthodox resistance to such change. The change itself can only be a monumental historic process. Thus speaking of the West he suggests that "the substance of the biblical faith will undergo so radical a change of language, preaching, and living practice that to the captives of traditional forms it may look like the end of ecclesiastic religion." PFR, p. 321.

[133] Such issues concerning the nature of knowledge, the knowledge of nature, and the separation of freedom from knowledge and nature in the idea of history have already been suggested in various footnotes. They all, in one way or another, revolve around the question of the adequacy of the Kantian understanding

of both subjectivity and objectivity, and the consequent possibility of founding metaphysics and/or religion upon that understanding of subject and object.

[134] R., p. 779.

[135] VdW, p. 635.

[136] On this view, then, the Enlightenment's opposition of natural and positive religion at least recognized real differences (or plurality) which in fact disappear in Jaspers' seductively deceptive affirmation of plurality whereby the movement of transcending Existenz is the deep or true element in all particular, historic truth claims.

[137] More fundamentally, of course, it is the status of the world as nature, object, and events--the entire realm which Jaspers calls "existence"--and the relation of the subject to such "otherness" which is at issue. Thus the pursuit of specific questions concerning Jaspers' affirmation of religious plurality finally leads, as noted above, to more general questions about the adequacy of the Kantian understanding of subjectivity and objectivity around which his foundational thinking is constructed.

[138] H. Barth (pp. 284-285) puts the same point somewhat differently in noting that for Jaspers only one historic particularity is crucial, namely the particular vision of autonomous humanity characteristic of 19th Century German idealism.

[139] Cf. Hans Urs von Balthasar's critique of Jaspers' intolerance in *The God Question and Modern Man* (New York: The Seabury Press, 1967), pp. 84-86.

[140] The question of mediation is evidently a complex one involving differing positions within as well as among religions. Inwardness, moreover, would certainly seem to be an essential characteristic of religious truth by most accounts. Still, as Jaspers himself stresses (R, pp. 778-779), it is the positive mediation of event, text, and tradition, of community and cult, "as the actuality of something specifically holy in places, objects, and acts" which distinguishes religion and makes witness and reverence specifically religious attitudes. Yet even this stress on religious positivity is less significant than it might seem. As H. Barth notes (pp. 292-293) Jaspers lumps all religious particularity indifferently together under general headings of "rite" and "dogma" and the like. The actual particularity or positivity of different religions is rarely, if ever, considered.

CHAPTER IV

NOTES

[1]Focus on the topic of historicity is appropriate not only because of its evident importance in Jaspers' thinking as well as in the preceding sections of this presentation of that thinking, but also because of the centrality of history to the question of religious pluralism and truth. Not only is religious plurality a fact arising from human history, but that contemporary consciousness of such plurality which provides the problematic context for the present discussion of religious truth is itself a manifestation of what might more generally (albeit too loosely) be called "modern historical consciousness."

[2]The charge comes not only from religious thinkers, but in different ways from thinkers concerned with a variety of topics. Transcending Existenz, it is said, loses the world, concrete history, the human community and the realities of politics and religion. Cf., for instance, the articles by Herbert Marcuse (pp. 131-132), Karl Löwith (pp. 149-152), and Otto Friedrich Bollnow (pp. 236-237), as well as the already noted articles by Jürgen Habermas (pp. 314-315) and Heinrich Barth (pp. 290-291) in Saner, ed., *Karl Jaspers in der Discussion.*

[3]Ph II, p. 106; cf. pp. 182-183, 295-297, 310.

[4]Ph II, p. 5; cf. pp. 257, 306.

[5]Dufrenne and Ricoeur, p. 66.

[6]To be sure, Jaspers' attitude toward mysticism is complex. He recognizes real differences veiled by the one term (PFR, p. 280) and finds some testimony to mysticism indubitably authentic (PFR, pp. 265 ss.; VdW, pp. 137, 702). Still, although mysticism as much as the religious faith with which it is so often connected is finally a polar other which Jaspers' thought does not comprehend, he struggles against mysticism because he "cannot bridge the chasm between man and God" (PFR, p. 264) and because mysticism (and religion) denies and finally loses the world (Ph II, pp. 277-279; cf. p. 183 and PFR, p. 25). For a discussion of Jaspers on mysticism, cf. Ehrlich, pp. 40-56.

The complexity of Jaspers' attitude toward mysticism is a good concrete illustration of his understanding of plurality and truth--where, in light of what one believes to be true, one struggles against, yet finally accepts the possible but uncomprehended truth of the other. Yet it is also worth noting that Jaspers' struggle against mysticism is in large measure a response to the view, as in the line of questioning under consideration here, which finds that his own thinking in fact ends in a type of world-losing mysticism. For a recent example of this view cf. Fritz Buri, "Concerning the Relationship of Philosophical Faith and Christian Faith," *Journal of the American Academy of Religion*, XL #4 (Dec., 1972), p. 455.

[7]Cf. above, p. 35.

[8]Cf., above all, *The Origin and Goal of History*; Ph II, pp. 104-129, 184-193, 342-359; and R, pp. 760-777. For interpretation, cf. especially the already cited article by Heinrich Barth, as well as John Hennig, "Karl Jaspers' Attitude Towards History," and Jeanne Hersch, "Jaspers' Conception of Tradition," both in Schilpp, pp. 565-593 and 593-610.

[9]The simplest summary of his ideas is the brief chapter on history in WW, pp. 96-109.

[10]That such historic situatedness constitutes the basic boundary situation has already been noted in the preceding chapter. Cf. above, pp. 59-60. The phrase "vertigo of relativity" is borrowed from Peter Berger, *A Rumor of Angels* (Garden City, NY: Doubleday, 1969), p. 40.

[11]Of course, the very affirmation of the historicist position is self-contradicting since it asserts as a-historically true that all truth claims are historical. Yet, although it is logically contradictory when expressed propositionally, historicism as a mood or attitude does express the climate of much contemporary thought which, aware of the historic situatedness of thought, finds no way beyond such situational relativity.

[12]Cf. pp. 24-26.

[13]R, p. 764. This, of course, is the point of Lessing's remark that "an ugly broad ditch which I cannot get across, however often and however earnestly I have tried to make the leap," separates the "accidental truths of history" from the absolute truth claimed by religion. Cf. *Lessing's Theological Writings*, ed. Owen Chadwick (London: Adam and Charles Black, 1956), pp. 55, 53.

[14]Ph II, p. 347.

[15]Ph II, p. 348. It is perhaps worth observing again that here, even more so than in his general discussion of knowledge in terms of scientific knowing, Jaspers does not argue but takes for granted this critique of knowledge. His primary concern is with the possibility of truth in the situation resulting from the critique.

[16]For Jaspers historicity and communication are inseparable. Communication at the level of Existenz is not, for him, a royal (if rough) road to harmony, but a loving struggle with real otherness which throws one back upon oneself in awareness of one's historicity. For Jaspers it is, as will be seen below, the context or way for the attainment of absolute truth, but only because it first is the context which concretely awakens one to the boundary of one's own situatedness. For Jaspers' understanding of communication, cf. above all Ph II, pp. 47-103, as well as RE, pp. 77-106.

[17]Ph II, p. 346.

[18]Ph II, p. 346.

[19]Ph III, p. 11.

[20]It is a tragic irony of our times that the more we claim to know about the past, the less we seem capable of serious links with it. Traditional man, who perhaps knew relatively little in terms of our ideal of historical accuracy, lived in deep continuity with the past, while the children of the present increasingly find the "dead" past unearthed for them by the scholar's toil "irrelevant" to their living concerns.

[21]Ph II, pp. 347, 346.

[22]Cf. above, pp. 37-38.

[23]Ph III, p. 26. Cf. VdW, pp. 909-913.

[24]R, pp. 761-765. This of course is the charge which Jaspers makes against religion generally, but above all against the Christian idea of revelation. Cf. PFR, pp. 100-102. Jaspers, as will be seen below, continually uses the notion of "embodiment" to contrast with the idea of "cipher" in terms of which he understands the contents of particular, historic realizations of transcendence.

[25]Ph II, pp. 116, 348-349, and OGH, especially pp. 267-269. Sketches of the unity of history, such as Jaspers' own are quite legitimate as elements in the process of existential elucidation, but become false and terrible when taken as knowable masterplans into which the diversity of history is to be forced. Jaspers' primary target here is Marxist orthodoxy. Cf. RAR, pp. 8-20.

[26]RAR, pp. 20-27.

[27]VdW, pp. 847-857.

[28]Ph III, p. 26.

[29]VdW, p. 849. As regards present reappropriation of traditions, for instance, Jaspers stresses that "only emancipation from this required obedience will bring the individual so to himself" that "existential commitment without the fixed form of tradition" will be possible. Ph III, p. 26.

[30]Ph II, p. 108.

[31]Ph II, p. 116.

[32]Evidently the present account of Jaspers' response is an interpretative reconstruction drawn from various parts of his writings. Still it is true to say that *his* response begins with such negation because this is the invariable pattern of his dialectic, a pattern dictated by the Kantian framework of his thought.

[33]Because the threat of nihilism is "the acid in which the gold of truth must be proved," its ever present danger provides "a transition to a profounder assimilation of historic tradition." PSP, p. 173.

[34]Thus Paul Ricoeur's repeated accusation that the weight of Jaspers' thinking carries him, despite his protestations to the contrary, into "the non-commitment of aestheticism"--"like a Don Juan courting all the gods," but finally standing aloof observing the panorama of history's (ever-relative) abundance. Schilpp, pp. 638-639; cf. Dufrenne and Ricoeur, p. 391.

[35]There is, Jaspers notes, "no way round history, but only a way through history," OGH, p. 275. The correlation of limitation and depth, or the idea of "profundity only in narrowness," is, as Jean Wahl notes, one of the basic experiences governing all of Jaspers' thought. *La Pensée de l'Existence*, p. 64.

[36]PW, p. 150.

[37]Ph II, pp. 104-105. For Jaspers, unlike others who have later used it, the distinction never solidifies into two realms--"*Historie*" and "*Geschichte*." There is only one reality, approached now as an object of knowledge and again as a possibility of serious, existential appropriation. Even as regards terminology Jaspers is, as noted, almost deliberately imprecise, generally using the term "*Geschichte*" for all of the various senses of history.

[38]Ph II, p. 105.

[39]Ph II, p. 106.

[40]Ph I, p. 264; VdW, pp. 651-652; PSP, pp. 4-5.

[41]PSP, p. 4. Jaspers elsewhere (PFR, p. 46) calls Bruno "the great martyr of modern philosophy" for his stand in personal faith against the violently exclusive claims of religious "catholicism."

[42]PSP, p. 4.

[43]PSP, p. 4. (Emphasis added.)

[44]Jaspers does speak of Bruno as a "great metaphysician" whose thinking has influenced his own. Ph I, p. 2. Yet he admits that "the saints of philosophy" are not necessarily the greatest philosophers. PSP, p. 5.

[45]In this context one may readily think of two other figures from the same period who have been seen as exemplars of such existential commitment in much recent literature--Thomas More and Martin Luther. Indeed Luther's "Here I stand!" might well serve as a motto for Jaspers' idea of historicity. Jaspers' failure to mention either probably stems in part from his primary concern with philosophical, and not religious faith,

and in part from the fact that Luther seems to him the embodiment of that intolerant religious exclusivism against which his idea of existential historicity is aimed. Cf. PFR, p. 46.

[46]Once again, of course, what follows is a brief reconstruction of a typical pattern of Jaspers' thinking on the idea of historicity and not an attempt to follow the complex and rich detail of that thinking.

[47]Ph II, pp. 346-351, 114-118, 124-129. In addition to the already discussed absolutization of a particular present, Jaspers mentions romantic flight to the past, aesthetic contemplation of historic diversity, or simple indifference--all unexistential attitudes because in each the possibility of Existenz is lost.

[48]Ph II, p. 118.

[49]Ph II, pp. 191-192.

[50]Ph II, pp. 93-95.

[51]Ph II, p. 192.

[52]The first part of that "Existential Elucidation" to which the entire second (and central) volume of *Philosophy* is devoted is called "I Myself in Communication and Historicity." Major primary sources for Jaspers' discussion of communication are the lengthy chapter in *Philosophy* (II, pp. 47-103) and RE, pp. 77-106.

[53]Ph II, pp. 47-51, 61-63; RE, pp. 80-85, 94-95.

[54]Ph II, pp. 51-54; RE, pp. 85-91.

[55]Ph II, pp. 93-95, 81-82. One of Jaspers' continual charges against religious faith is its refusal of communication in the name of a revealed truth to be followed in strict obedience rather than in the openness of communication. Cf. Ph II, pp. 57-58; PSP, p. 77, and PFR, *passim*.

[56]Ph II, p. 93.

[57]Ph II, p. 53. (Emphasis added.)

[58]OMP, p. 147.

[59]RE, pp. 104-106. More generally, communicability is a keynote of each of the meanings of truth in the different modes of the encompassing--"what is common to all truth in all modes of the encompassing: that to be generally true, truth must be communicable." RE, p. 77.

[60]RE, p. 104.

[61]Ph II, pp. 63-64.

[62]RE, p. 104.

[63]Ph II, p. 63.

[64]Ph II, p. 106.

[65]Ph II, p. 69.

[66]Ph II, p. 362.

[67]Jaspers singles out von Ranke's philosophy of history as an example of this widespread position. Ph II, p. 113.

[68]Ph II, p. 362.

[69]Ph II, p. 108.

[70]Ph II, p. 117.

[71]Ph II, p. 363.

[72]Ph II, p. 192.

[73]Ph II, p. 192. (Emphasis added.)

[74]Ph II, pp. 105, 108.

[75]Ph II, p. 108.

[76]Ph II, p. 181.

[77]For an excellent account of Jaspers' thinking about tradition, cf. the already cited article by Jeanne Hersch in Schilpp, pp. 593-610, and Jaspers' "Reply," pp. 760-777.

[78]R, p. 776.

[79]The image is Hersch's, p. 595. Cf. Ph II, p. 116.

[80]Ph II, p. 118; cf. pp. 111-114 (on continuity) and 118-120 (on fidelity).

[81]Jaspers' lengthy discussions of authority constitute a major theme in his thought. Cf. VdW, pp. 766-831; PE, pp. 47-53, and the article "Liberty and Authority" in PW, pp. 33-56.

[82]*La Pensée de l'Existence*, pp. 104-105.

[83]Ph III, p. 23. Jaspers immediately adds, of course, that "this very unconditionality would make it shun any exclusiveness and any claim to universality." It is absolute precisely as historic.

[84]Ph II, p. 109: It "is no procurement of an extant, enunciable possession."

[85]Here and in what follows the term "moment" should not be misunderstood. Jaspers contrasts the transcending awareness in "the exalted moment," the moment of unconditional act wherein

Existenz is aware of transcendence, with the timeless, unhistoric validity of knowledge. But this moment is part ("both culmination and articulation") of the "historic succession of interrelated moments"--the process, for instance, of communication, or the gradual growth of freedom and responsibility over time. Cf. Ph II, pp. 110-113.

[86]Cf. Ph II, p. 105 and the entire section of VdW entitled "*Wahrheit im Durchbruch*," pp. 710 ss., especially 710-745.

[87]Ph II, p. 107.

[88]Cf. Ph III, pp. 18-19.

[89]VdW, p. 651. Eternity, for Jaspers, is not a changeless realm, "somewhere else, aside from temporal appearance" (Ph II, p. 113), but the fullness of realization in time, "the overcoming of time within time" (VdW, p. 651.).

[90]Ph II, p. 111.

[91]Ph II, pp. 111, 306.

[92]Ph II, p. 107.

[93]Ph II, p. 107.

[94]Ph II, p. 109.

[95]Tilliette (p. 63) even calls it "the masterpiece of his metaphysical thinking."

[96]The major primary sources are Ph III, pp. 113-208, VdW, pp. 1022-1054 (published separately in English as *Truth and Symbol*) and PFR, pp. 92-127. In addition to the particular chapters in the already-cited secondary sources by Dufrenne and Ricoeur, Ehrlich, Samay, and Tilliette, there have been numerous articles and studies devoted particularly to the significance of Jaspers' idea of cipher for the understanding of religion. Recent and noteworthy is Aloys Klein, *Glaube und Mythos* (München: Verlag Ferdinand Schöningh, 1973).

[97]Cf. above, pp. 66-67.

[98]VdW, p. 1022. The passage illustrates Jaspers' deliberate terminological imprecision. Generally, however, he speaks of "cipher" rather than "symbol" (the use of metaphor in this context being quite rare) because symbol too often suggests that there is something else which could be known directly, outside the symbol. PFR, p. 95. Cf. Ph III, pp. 123-131 for Jaspers' early effort to locate his idea of cipher within a more general understanding of symbolism.

[99]PFR, p. 93.

[100]PFR, p. 93.

[101]Cf. PFR, p. 95. (The phrase from Gerard Manley Hopkins is not cited by Jaspers but does seem to express his meaning.)

[102]Ph III, pp. 114-115.

[103]In view of remarks made in the preceding chapter about Jaspers' dark view of nature or world, it is worth nothing here that the world which *literally* held no word for man in answer to his fundamental questions might still *as cipher* function as the language of transcendence. The shift from consciousness-at-large to Existenz, in other words, enables men "to find the right way into the world" (Ph II, p. 5), to "experience the world as the language of God...the meeting point of that which is eternal and that which manifests itself in time" (PSP, p. 36). In Ehrlich's phrase (p. 253, n. 4), the world functions to "mediate the immediacy" of existential relation to transcendence. On ciphers of nature, understood more specifically as the natural world, cf. Ph III, pp. 152-159 and PFR, pp. 96-98, 168-186.

[104]MC, p. 16.

[105]Ph III, pp. 115-119.

[106]Philosophy, then, is as much a thinking in ciphers as myth and religion. It does not provide a method of demythologizing or a key to the real (literal, sole) meaning of the ciphers. Myth and religion are not, in other words, transformed into their true substance as philosophy. Rather myth and religion and philosophy each provide an authentic possibility or way in the world of ciphers. This, of course, is the basic point in Jaspers' critique of Bultmann. Cf. MC, pp. 15 ss.

[107]The reading of ciphers is not deciphering in the sense of movement from cipher to the real or literal meaning somehow behind the cipher. Such deciphering is, for Jaspers, clearly impossible. All interpretation of ciphers remains a thinking in ciphers and thus can never be final. "The essence of what a cipher is can be stated only in another cipher." PFR, p. 116.

[108]PSP, pp. 111-117.

[109]PFR, p. 95.

[110]PFR, p. 96.

[111]PFR, pp. 100 ss. Here again, in only slightly altered form, is Jaspers' continual critique of "catholicism" as the unwarranted claim to know what cannot be known. In PFR, of course, the Christian doctrine of revelation as Jaspers understands it is the particular form of embodiment under attack.

[112]PFR, p. 100.

[113]PFR, p. 124.

[114]Cf. PFR, pp. 109, 145-148, 161-164.

[115]PFR, pp. 125-126.

[116]PFR, pp. 119, 121, 127.

[117]PSP, p. 11. Cf. Jean Wahl, *La Pensée de l'Existence*, p. 127.

[118]It is not Rome alone, nor even Christian orthodoxy generally, but religious orthodoxy in any form which here stands accused of the "Babylonian captivity" of true faith.

[119]Cf. the previously cited work by Heinrich Fries for one of the more polemic rebuttals from the religious side.

[120]H. Barth, p. 292.

[121]Consider the following remark by the American theologian William Stringfellow in his "Introduction" to Daniel Berrigan's *They Call Us Dead Men* (NY: Macmillan, 1966), p. 11: "This book is not religious in the conventional sense of that term: it does not expound dogma; it does not resort to jargon; it upholds no ritualistic vanities...it does not cater to the lust for indulgences; it does not assault the conscience, nor does it insult intelligence."

[122]The most recently published example of that continued interest is the study of *Gotteserfahrung und Glaube* by Helmut Pfeiffer (Trier: Paulinus-Verlag, 1975). The work is subtitled *Interpretation und Theologische Aneignung der Philosophie Karl Jaspers'* ("interpretation *and* theological appropriation"). The present study is likewise, of course, evidence of such continued interest.

[123]The work of Xavier Tilliette would be the most noteworthy example, but the concern to reformulate faith in ways understandable to "modern man" is evidently a preoccupation of much contemporary theological work.

[124]PFR, p. 322.

[125]PFR, pp. 231 ss.; PSP, pp. 95 ss.

[126]In this context Jaspers remarks, quite sincerely it would seem: "How oddly disproportionate it is for an individual to write about such things! How infinitesmal his thinking looks against the overwhelming sweep of history and its spiritual forces." PFR, p. 322.

[127]PSP, pp. 96, 103; PFR, p.322.

[128]PSP, pp. 108-109.

[129]PFR, pp. 100 ss., 337 ss.

[130]Cf. PFR, pp. 329-356; PSP, pp. 82-112.

[131]PFR, p. 330.

[132]PSP, p. 109.

[133]PFR, pp. 339-342.

[134]PFR, pp. 330-337.

[135]VdW, pp. 1052-1053; PFR, pp. 337-339.

[136]PSP, pp. 104-106; PFR, pp. 342-343.

[137]PFR, p. 101; cf. p. 103: "The great question is whether anything stripped of corporeality can remain effective as a mere cipher."

[138]PFR, pp. 353, 321, 329.

[139]PFR, p. 101. Cf., p. 112: "Where worship was regarded as cipher it seemed it could be solemn and serious in freedom, weighty in suspension, without loss of vigour." Jaspers' protestantism is evident in this approach to the sacramental. In historical terms, he clearly sides with Zwingli against Luther and Catholicism.

[140]While the issues in the famous Jaspers-Bultmann debate are complex, it is fairly accurate to say that Jaspers disagrees with Bultmann at two fundamental points. And these points not only serve to summarize Jaspers' understanding of religious truth, but testify to the seriousness of his concern for specifically religious positivity. In the first place, as would be expected, he attacks Bultmann's rigid, exclusivist orthodoxy. Despite all the pseudo-liberalism of Bultmann's program, it finally proclaims the one Christian truth as *the* saving truth for all men. Secondly, however, he attacks the demythologizing program because it robs Christianity of precisely that rich particular world of ciphers by means of which it might serve as a vehicle of faith. It impoverishes religion in the name of the pseudo-scientific world-view of modern man. Cf. MC, *passim*; R, pp. 782-783.

[141]PFR, p. 88.

[142]PSP, p. 181. Cf. RE, pp. 100-103.

[143]WW, p. 106.

[144]Cf. PFR, pp. 356-363; 321-322.

CHAPTER V

NOTES

[1]Although it sounds a bit grandiose, one might well refer to the type of thinking here as "modern" (Kantian or post-Kantian) and thus to its effort to resolve the problem of pluralism and truth as "the modern project," or at least "a modern project," concerning religious pluralism. That Jaspers, at least, wants to understand his thinking in those terms should be clear from introductory remarks in Chapter I (esp. pp. 13-15) and the entire discussion of Chapter II.

[2]Cf., for instance, Tilliette, pp. 120 ss., or Klein, pp. 216-234 (where recent theological discussion of Jaspers is reviewed).

[3]*God's Presence in History* (New York: New York University Press, 1970), pp. 8-11, 30.

[4]John Hick, *Philosophy of Religion*, p. 128.

[5]Cf. Charles Davis, *Christ and the World Religions*, pp. 26-39 and the chapter on "Religious Symbolism and 'Universal' Religion" in Maurice Friedmann's *Touchstones of Reality* (New York: E. P. Dutton, 1974), pp. 216-233. Friedmann (p. 226) cites Abraham Heschel's pointed observation that "in earlier times, symbolism was regarded as a form of *religious thinking*. In modern times religion is regarded as a *form of symbolic thinking*."

[6]Although not focused in exactly this way, Jaspers makes essentially the same argument in his "Reply to My Critics" in Schilpp. Cf. R, pp. 777-785.

[7]PSP, p. 77, and CM, p. 112 (I have used parts of each translation of the same passage).

[8]The two approaches ("from outside" and "from within") should actually meet and overlap since the basic issues involved would finally be the same.

[9]Cf. above, p. 18.

[10]Cf. above, p 42.

[11]The confusion of the two senses of dialectic, of the intended holding together with the actual transformation, is, I think, at least part of the explanation for the ambiguity one often feels in reading Jaspers, the sense that, as noted above, the pieces of the puzzle seem to be there, yet somehow not put together correctly. And Jaspers' language, talk of "mediated immediacy" for instance, serves only to heighten such confusion--perhaps even for Jaspers himself.

[12]This critique would not, of course, mean that the actual (as distinct from the intended) achievement of Jaspers' thought is wrong. The existential logic of faith which is described by Jaspers' philosophy may well be correct even if it does not provide a basis for affirming the possibility of a plurality of true religions.

[13]Cf. above, pp. 10, 12, 17, 24-25.

[14]The word "object" is here used only in the broadest sense to refer to that transcendence which, *in se* non-objectifiable, is the goal or object of religious affirmation. It might, of course, be conceptualized, even within the same tradition, in either subjective or objective categories (e.g., *Atman* and *Brahman*).

[15]Not only does most analysis of religion contain some similar sort of qualification about the character of "God talk," but the actual usage of the various traditions, I think it could be shown, is on the whole equally careful to balance affirmation with negation.

[16]Once again, I am not here arguing that religious truth is in fact most adequately understood in terms of the first sense of particularity, but only that the attempt to resolve the problem of pluralism and truth by affirming the possibility of a plurality of true religions must somehow involve this sense of particularity.

[17]Cf. Jean Wahl, *La Pensée de l'Existence*, pp. 130-131: With Kierkegaard Jaspers stresses that existential truth is not a matter of content but of the character of quality of relation (not "what" but "how").

[18]The point here is relevant not only for the formal beliefs of the different religious traditions, but also for more directly personal religious experiences. Thus, as noted above, Jaspers could well agree with Hopkins that "the world is charged with the grandeur of God." (Cf. GP:O, pp. 251-252.) Yet what he would mean would not, I think, be exactly what the poet meant. For on Jaspers' terms it is not strictly speaking the world, or things and events in the world, which is "charged with the grandeur of God." (Even if it were, we could not know that to be the case.) Rather the world, or objects and events in the world, might serve or function as cipher, as an occasion for the transcending awareness of Existenz.

[19]PFR, p. 92.

[20]The predominance of negation in the movement of Jaspers' dialectic can also be seen in the fundamental importance for him of the notions of "foundering" and "failure" and "shipwreck," and the corresponding importance of metaphors of "transcending" and "breakthrough." Cf. Johannes Thyssen, "The Concept of 'Foundering' in Jaspers' Philosophy" in Schilpp, pp. 297-335.

[21]Ph III, p. 23 (cf. above, p. 93).

[22]Ph II, p. 109 (cf. above, p. 95).

[23]PFR, p. 92.

[24]Essentially the same argument about the priority of function over content in Jaspers' analysis of the logic of existential truth could be made in terms of Jaspers' idea of *communication*. Truth, he insists, can be attained only in communication and, just as in the case of ciphers, such communication necessarily involves particular contents and commitments. Once again, however, it is not the communicated contents, but the process itself, precisely in its failure to arrive at finally communicable content, which becomes the medium of truth. The "loving struggle" of communication, in other words, is itself the dialectic which brings those contents into suspension thereby establishing the possibility of existential transcending. Cf. above, p. 90.

[25]I have here argued that there is no room for the type of plurality in Jaspers which would be needed to resolve the pluralism and truth dilemma by examining the character of that particularity and plurality which are in fact sustained by his argument. Another more fundamentally direct approach would have been to argue that, once again his own protestations to the contrary notwithstanding, the contents of Jaspers' philosophy are not themselves matters of faith but assertions which claim the status of knowledge. Put differently, what he asserts about transcendence and our relations to transcendence are cognitive assertions which make particular, universal claims and exclude opposing claims. For the beginnings of such an argument, cf. the important article by William Earle, "Jaspers' Philosophical Anthropology" in Schilpp, pp. 523-538.

[26]*Op. cit.*, pp. 284-285; 290-291; cf. 275-276, 278.

[27]*Ibid.*, pp. 281-282.

[28]What follows is less an argument than a series of related observations and implications flowing from the preceding argument. The points made could, I believe, be argued in detail but that is not attempted here.

[29]Cf. above, pp. 72-74, 75, 100ss, 102.

[30]Cf. above, p. 102.

[31]R, p. 779.

[32]PFR, p. 92.

[33]Cf. Ph I, p. 88; PFR, pp. 258-261.

[34]Such is Tilliette's (p. 131) critique of Jaspers.

[35]Friedmann, *Touchstones of Reality*, p. 232.

[36]R, pp. 777-779.

[37]R, p. 778.

[38]*Op. cit.*, pp. 334-335.

[39]R, pp. 778-779.

[40]*Surprised by Joy* (New York: Harcourt, Brace and World, 1955), p. 210. A remarkably similar account is presented in the autobiographical writings of Martin Buber. Cf. "Eine Bekehrung" in *Begegnung: Autobiographische Fragmente* (Stuttgart: W. Kohlhammer Verlag, 1961), pp. 36-38.

[41]Even so severe a critic as Karl Barth can stress the positive significance of Jaspers' thought insofar as it continually points to man's fundamental openness to the reality of transcendence. Cf. "Phänomene des Menschlichen" in Saner, ed., *Karl Jaspers in der Discussion*, pp. 319 ss.

[42]George Grant, *Time as History* (Toronto: Canadian Broadcasting Corporation, 1969), p. 29.

[43]Cf. PSP, pp. 100-107; PFR, pp. 330-337, 355-356.

[44]"Introduction," to Jaspers' *The European Spirit*, p. 17.

[45]It is Paul Ricoeur (in Schilpp, p. 639) who thus turns Kierkegaard's image against Jaspers.

[46]Jeanne Hersch, p. 604.

[47]Jaspers' views on the dependence of philosophy upon the more "sociologically effective transmission" of the contents of faith by the religions have already been noted (cf. PSP, p. 112), as has Heinrich Barth's judgment (*Op. cit.*, p. 279) that the power and appeal of Jaspers' thought derive from the continued presence in it of the earlier traditions of Western thought and belief. In this regard, Jeanne Hersch (pp. 603-604), developing the Trojan horse metaphor, notes that "perhaps all of us--and more than anyone Jaspers in whom is incarnated... a whole tradition--are like the children of rich men who live *unknowingly* off a still sumptuous inheritance (while we think it already exhausted). Perhaps we are going to leave our descendants a misery far deeper than we can ever imagine." (Emphasis added.)

[48]There is, of course, an alternative explanation: Jaspers' account of particularity is not at all the best account, nor even one of the better accounts possible on these foundations. There have, in fact, been far better accounts of particularity, and specifically of religious particularity, which have been developed in terms of essentially the same (Kantian or idealist) foundations. Thus Jaspers' failure is not representative and does not indicate the need for some fundamentally different approach to thought about religious pluralism.

Those who might be persuaded somewhat by the preceding critique of Jaspers, but who nonetheless find significant resources for thought about religious truth in the work of others (Tillich, for instance) who build on essentially the same foundations, would understand Jaspers' failure in some such terms. For my part, I am suggesting that Jaspers' failure is, in fact, fully understood only in terms of this inadequacy of the foundations of his thought, and that this failure would thus also be found in those who share these same foundations. My position would have to be argued, of course, either by examining the specific accounts of religious truth provided by those other thinkers or by showing, and not simply suggesting, that there is something fundamentally inimical to an adequate account of particularity in this whole approach to the question of religious truth.

[49]In his book *Christ and Apollo* (New York: Mentor-Omega, 1963), pp. 23-26, theologian and literary critic William Lynch explores various essentially negative "attitudes toward the finite" or "images of the finite" which quite closely parallel aspects of the significance of the objective in Jaspers' thought. There are, firstly, those imaginations which "try to achieve a tenuous, mystical contact with the finite, touching it just sufficiently...to produce mystical vision, but not solidly enough...for their vision to be impaired by the actuality of things." They use the concretely real as "a sort of resilient, rubbery surface off which to rebound as quickly as possible into various parts of the sky." Then there are those who "desire to touch the finite as lightly as possible in order to rebound, not into a quick eternity...but back into the self." And finally there are those whose imagination "penetrates, at least to some degree, into our human flesh and environment," but then recoils from the fundamental darkness it finds, and "flies, in a second movement that is unrelated to the first and constitutes an act of rebellion and escape, into a tenuous world of infinite bliss." None of these types, of course, exactly fits Jaspers, but the parallels do, I think, illuminate his more abstractly worded understanding (or image) of the objective and illustrate in turn the extent to which his understanding is not at all atypical.

[50]I personally find, for instance, that Maurice Friedmann's attempt to totally jettison the language of symbolism and to understand religious truth in terms of "touchstones of reality" is quite promising. Cf. *Touchstones of Reality*, esp. pp. 21-29, 216-233.

BIBLIOGRAPHY

What follows is not a complete bibliography of works consulted for the present study, and much less a bibliography of available literature on the topic of the study. It is, rather, a listing under various headings of all works cited and of all other key works actually used in the preparation of this study.

For a more complete bibliography of Jaspers' works see Klaus Piper, ed., *Karl Jaspers: Werk und Wirkung* (München: R. Piper and Co. Verlag, 1963) which contains the most complete published bibliography. It includes information on Jaspers' works (and on many translations) by year until 1962, but its compiler now notes that it "contains quite a few errors" (letter from Hans Saner, Basel, February 10, 1974). A corrected version of this bibliography, updated through 1972, has been prepared for the announced, but to my knowledge not yet published second German edition of P. A. Schilpp, ed., *Karl Jaspers* (originally published in 1957 by W. Kohlhammer Verlag, Stuttgart and simultaneously in English by Tudor Publishing Company, New York and containing an earlier version of the bibliography which appears in *Karl Jaspers: Werk und Wirkung*). An extensive and critical "Primär-Bibliographie" has been prepared for separate publication by Karl Kunert and Gisela Gefken (Landesbibliothek, Oldenburg), but no publisher has yet been found. They have also collected material for an extensive "Sekundär-Bibliographie" which as of mid-1974 contained over ten thousand titles arranged under various topic headings. An account of Jaspers' unpublished manuscripts is given by Hans Saner, his literary executor, in "Zu Karl Jaspers' Nachlass" in Hans Saner, ed., *Karl Jaspers in der Discussion* (München: R. Piper & Company Verlag, 1973) pp. 449-463.

While the secondary literature on Jaspers, even as it relates only to his thought about religious questions, is immense, there are fairly extensive and representative bibliographies in the works listed below (section 2) by Klein, Pfeiffer, and Samay.

1. Works by Karl Jaspers

Each item is listed according to the edition and/or translation actually used, with additional information given about the original source in the case of later editions and translations. (As noted above in the Preface, where the translation of any passage seemed doubtful, it has been checked against the original.) Works referred to throughout by means of abbreviations are here preceded by those abbreviations.

CT *Chiffren der Transzendenz*. Ed. by Hans Saner. 2nd. ed. München: R. Piper & Co. Verlag, 1972. Text of 1961 course lectures, first published in 1970.

The European Spirit. Trans. by R. G. Smith. London: SCM, 1948. 1946 lecture delivered at the Rencontres Internationales de Geñeve and first published in *L'Esprit Européen, Recontres Internationales de Genève 1946* (Paris: 1946), 291-323.

EH *Existentialism and Humanism: Three Essays*. Trans. by E. G. Ashton. New York: Russell F. Moore Co., 1952. Articles originally published separately--"Unsere Zukunft und Goethe" in 1947, "Solon" in 1948, and "Über Bedingungen und Möglichkeiten eines neuen Humanismus" in 1949--and collected along with other articles and speeches in *Rechenschaft und Ausblick* (München: R. Piper & Co. Verlag, 1951).

GP:F *The Great Philosophers: The Foundations*. Ed. by Hannah Arendt. Trans. by R. Manheim. New York: Harcourt, Brace, and World, Inc., 1962. Originally published as part of *Die grossen Philosophen, I* (München: R. Piper & Co. Verlag, 1957).

GP:O *The Great Philosophers: The Original Thinkers*. Ed. by Hannah Arendt. Trans. by R. Manheim. New York: Harcourt, Brace, and World, Inc., 1962. Originally published as two separate works: as part of *Die grossen Philosophen, I* (München: R. Piper & Co. Verlag, 1957) and as *Nikolaus Cusanus* (München: R. Piper & Co. Verlag, 1964).

"The Importance of Kierkegaard," trans. by E. W. Geissman, *Cross Currents* 2 (1951-52), 5-16. A 1951 lecture first published as "Kierkegaard--Leben und Werk" in *Universitas*, VI #1 (Stuttgart, 1951),1057-1070.

"The Importance of Nietzsche, Marx, and Kierkegaard in the History of Philosophy," trans. by S. Godman, *The Hibbert Journal* 49 (1950-51), 226-234. Article originally published as "Zu Nietzsche's Bedeutung in der Geschichte der Philosophie" in *Die neue Rundschau*, LXI (Frankfurt am Main, 1950) 346-358.

Leonardo, Descartes, Max Weber: Three Essays. Trans. by R. Manheim. London: Routledge & Kegan Paul, 1965. Originally published as three separate works: *Lionardo als Philosoph* (Bern: Franke Verlag, 1953), *Descartes und die Philosophie* (Berlin: W. de Gruyter & Co., 1937), and *Max Weber: Deutsches Wesen im politischen Denken, im Forschen und Philosophieren* (Oldenburg i. O.: G. Stalling, 1932).

MMA *Man in the Modern Age*. Trans. by E. Paul and C. Paul. Garden City, New York: Doubleday & Co., Inc., 1957. First published as *Die geistige Situation der Zeit* (Berlin: W. de Gruyter & Co., 1931).

MC *Myth and Christianity*. With Rudolf Bultmann. Trans. by N. Guterman. New York: The Noonday Press, 1969. First published as *Die Frage der Entmythologisierung* (München: R. Piper & Co. Verlag, 1954).

"Nekrolog von Karl Jaspers selbst Verfasst," *Gedankenfeier für Karl Jaspers am 4 März 1969*. Basler Universitäts Reden, 60 Heft. Basel: Verlag Helbing und Lichtenhahn, 1969.

Nietzsche and Christianity. Trans. by E. B. Ashton. Chicago: Henry Regnery Co., 1951. Based on a lecture delivered in 1938; first published as *Nietzsche und das Christentum* (Hameln: Seifert, 1946).

OMP "On My Philosophy." Trans. by F. Kaufmann. In *Existentialism from Dostoevsky to Sartre*. Ed. by Walter Kaufmann. New York: Meridian Books, 1968, pp. 131-158. Essay first published in Italian translation in 1941, and first appearing in German as "Über meine Philosophie" in *Rechenschaft und Ausblick* (München: R. Piper & Co. Verlag, 1951).

OGH *The Origin and Goal of History*. Trans. by M. Bullock. New Haven: Yale University Press, 1968. First published as *Vom Ursprung und Ziel der Geschichte* (Zürich: Artemis, 1949).

PSP *The Perennial Scope of Philosophy*. Trans. by R. Manheim. Archon Books, 1968. 1947 lecture first published as *Der philosophische Glaube* (Zürich: Artemis, 1948).

PA "Philosophical Autobiography." Trans. by P. A. Schilpp and L. B. Lefebre. *The Philosophy of Karl Jaspers.* Ed. by P. A. Schilpp. New York: Tudor Publishing Co., 1957, pp. 5-94. Published simultaneously in German in P. A. Schilpp, ed., *Karl Jaspers* (Stuttgart: W. Kohlhammer Verlag, 1957).

PFR *Philosophical Faith and Revelation.* Trans. by E. B. Ashton. London: Collins, 1967. Translation of *Der philosophische Glaube angesichts der Offenbarung* (cf. below).

Philosophie. 3 vols. 3rd edition with a 1955 "Afterword." Berlin: Springer Verlag, 1956. First published in 1932.

PGO *Der philosophische Glaube angesichts der Offenbarung.* München: R. Piper & Co. Verlag, 1962.

Ph I, Ph II, Ph III *Philosophy.* 3 vols. Trans. of 3rd edition of *Philosophie* by E. B. Ashton. Chicago: The University of Chicago Press, 1969, 1970, 1971.

PW *Philosophy and the World.* Trans. by E. B. Ashton. Chicago: Henry Regnery Co., 1963. Partial translation of *Philosophie und Welt* (München: R. Piper & Co. Verlag, 1958), a collection of lectures and essays originally published between 1949 and 1957.

PE *Philosophy of Existence.* Trans. by R. F. Grabau. Philadelphia: University of Pennsylvania Press, 1971. 1937 lectures first published as *Existenzphilosophie* (Berlin: W. de Gruyter & Co., 1938).

Provokationen. Ed. by Hans Saner. München: R. Piper & Co. Verlag, 1969. A collection of interviews and conversations dating from 1960 through 1968.

RAR *Reason and Anti-Reason in Our Time.* Trans. by S. Godman. London: SCM, 1952. 1950 lectures published as *Vernunft und Widervernunft in unserer Zeit* (München: R. Piper & Co. Verlag, 1950).

RE *Reason and Existenz.* Trans. by W. Earle. New York: The Noonday Press, 1971. 1935 lectures published as *Vernunft und Existenz* (Groningen: Wolters, 1935).

R "Reply to my Critics." Trans. by P. A. Schilpp and L. B. Lefebre. *The Philosophy of Karl Jaspers.* Ed. by P. A. Schilpp. New York: Tudor Publishing Co., 1957, pp. 749-869. Published simultaneously in German in P. A. Schilpp, ed., *Karl Jaspers* (Stuttgart: W. Kohlhammer Verlag, 1957).

Schicksal und Wille: Autobiographische Schriften. Ed. by Hans Saner. München: R. Piper & Co. Verlag, 1967. A collection of autobiographical writings originally written in 1938, 1939-1942, 1966-1967, and 1967.

Tragedy Is Not Enough. Trans. by Harold A. T. Reiche, Harry T. Moore, and Karl W. Deutsch. Archon Books, 1969. A translation of *Von der Wahrheit*, pp. 915-961 (cf. below).

Truth and Symbol. Trans. by Jean T. Wilde, William Kluback, and William Kimmel. New Haven: College and University Press, 1959. A translation of *Von der Wahrheit*, pp. 1022-1054 (cf. below).

VdW *Von der Wahrheit.* München: R. Piper & Co. Verlag, 1958. First published in 1947.

Way to Wisdom: An Introduction to Philosophy. Trans. by R. Manheim. New Haven: Yale University Press, 1970. 1950 lectures published as *Einführung in die Philosophie* (Zürich: Artemis, 1950).

2. Secondary Literature on Jaspers' Philosophy

Arendt, Hannah. "Jaspers as Citizen of the World," in Schilpp, ed., *The Philosophy of Karl Jaspers*, pp. 539-549. New York: Tudor Publishing Co., 1957.

Balthasar, Hans Urs von. *The God Question and Modern Man.* Trans. by Hilda Graef. New York: The Seabury Press, 1967. First published in English as *Science, Religion, and Christianity* by Newman Press, Westminster, Maryland, 1958.

Barth, Heinrich. "Karl Jaspers über Glaube und Geschichte," in Hans Saner, ed., *Karl Jaspers in der Discussion*, pp. 274-296. München: R. Piper & Co. Verlag, 1973.

Barth, Karl. "Phänomene des Menschlichen," in *Kirchliche Dogmatik*, III/2, 128-143. Zürich: Zollikon, 1948. Also in Hans Saner, ed., *Karl Jaspers in der Discussion*, pp. 319-334. München: R. Piper & Co. Verlag, 1973.

Bollnow, Otto Friedrich. "Existenzphilosophie und Geschichte," in Hans Saner, ed., *Karl Jaspers in der Discussion*, pp. 235-273. München: R. Piper & Co. Verlag, 1973.

Buri, Fritz. "Concerning the Relationship of Philosophical Faith and Christian Faith," *Journal of the American Academy of Religion*, XL #4 (December 1972), 454-457.

Collins, James. "Jaspers on Science and Philosophy," in P. A. Schilpp, ed., *The Philosophy of Karl Jaspers*, pp. 115-140. New York: Tudor Publishing Co., 1957.

__________. "Philosophy of Existence and Positive Religion," *The Modern Schoolman*, XXIII #2 (January 1946), 82-100.

Dufrenne, Mikel, and Paul Ricoeur. *Karl Jaspers et la Philosophie de l'Existence*. Paris: Éditions de Seuil, 1947.

Earle, William. "Jaspers' Philosophical Anthropology," in P. A. Schilpp, ed., *The Philosophy of Karl Jaspers*, pp. 523-538. New York: Tudor Publishing Co., 1957.

Ehrlich, Leonard. *Karl Jaspers: Philosophy as Faith*. Amherst: The University of Massachusetts Press, 1975.

Fries, Heinrich. *Ist der Glaube ein Verrat am Menschen? Eine Begegnung mit Karl Jaspers*. Speyer: Pilger-Verlag, 1950.

Habermas, Jürgen. "Die Gestalten der Wahrheit," in Hans Saner, ed., *Karl Jaspers in der Discussion*, pp. 309-316. München: R. Piper & Co., Verlag, 1973.

Henning, John. "Karl Jaspers' Attitude Towards History," in P. A. Schilpp, ed., *The Philosophy of Karl Jaspers*, pp. 565-592. New York: Tudor Publishing Co., 1957.

Hersch, Jeanne. "Jaspers' Conception of Tradition," in P. A. Schilpp, ed., *The Philosophy of Karl Jaspers*, pp. 593-610. New York: Tudor Publishing Co., 1957.

Jonas, Hans. "Gnosticism, Existentialism, and Nihilism," in *The Gnostic Religion*, pp. 320-340. 2nd ed. Boston: Beacon Press, 1970.

Kaufmann, Walter. "Jaspers' Relation to Nietzsche," in P. A. Schilpp, ed., *The Philosophy of Karl Jaspers*, pp. 407-436. New York: Tudor Publishing Co., 1957.

Klein, Aloys. *Glaube und Mythos: Eine kritische, religionsphilosophisch-theologische Untersuchung des Mythos-Begriffs bei Karl Jaspers*. München: Verlag Ferdinand Schöningh, 1973.

Löwith, Karl. "Die geistige Situation der Zeit," in Hans Saner, ed., *Karl Jaspers in Der Discussion*, pp. 142-152. München: R. Piper & Co. Verlag, 1973.

__________. *Nature, History, and Existentialism*. Edited by Arnold Levison. Evanston: Northwestern University Press, 1966.

Lutz, T. J. von. *Reichweite und Grenzen von Karl Jaspers' Stellungnahme zu Religion und Offenbarung*. Dissertation, University of Munich, 1968.

Mann, Golo. "Freedom and the Social Sciences in Jaspers' Thought," in P. A. Schilpp, ed., *The Philosophy of Karl Jaspers*, pp. 551-564. New York: Tudor Publishing Co., 1957.

Marcel, Gabriel. "The Fundamental and the Ultimate Situation in Karl Jaspers," in *Creative Fidelity*, pp. 222-255. Trans. by Robert Rosthal. New York: Farrar, Strauss & Co., 1964.

Marcuse, Herbert. "Philosophie des Scheiterns," in Hans Saner, ed., *Karl Jaspers in Der Discussion*, pp. 125-132. München: R. Piper & Co. Verlag, 1973.

Mayer, Ernst. "Philosophie und philosophische Logik bei Jaspers," in Hans Saner, ed., *Karl Jaspers in Der Discussion*, pp. 224-232. München: R. Piper & Co. Verlag, 1973.

Pfeiffer, Helmut. *Gotteserfahrung und Glaube: Interpretation und theologische Aneignung der Philosophie Karl Jaspers'.* Trier: Paulinus Verlag, 1975.

Ricoeur, Paul. "The Relation of Jaspers' Philosophy to Religion," in P. A. Schilpp, ed., *The Philosophy of Karl Jaspers*, pp. 611-642. New York: Tudor Publishing Co., 1957.

Samay, Sebastian. *Reason Revisited: The Philosophy of Karl Jaspers.* Dublin: Gill and Macmillan, Ltd., 1971.

Saner, Hans. *Karl Jaspers.* Reinbeck bei Hamburg: Rowoholt, 1970.

__________, ed. *Karl Jaspers in der Discussion.* München: R. Piper & Co. Verlag, 1973.

__________. "Zu Karl Jaspers' Nachlass," in Hans Saner, ed., *Karl Jaspers in der Discussion*, pp. 449-463. München: R. Piper & Co. Verlag, 1973.

Schilpp, Paul Arthur, ed. *The Philosophy of Karl Jaspers.* New York: Tudor Publishing Co., 1957. (Published simultaneously in a German language edition by W. Kohlhammer-Verlag, Stuttgart.)

Schneiders, Werner von. *Karl Jaspers in der Kritik.* Bonn: H. Bouvier u. Co. Verlag, 1965.

Schrag, Oswald. *Existence, Existenz, and Transcendence: An Introduction to the Philosophy of Karl Jaspers.* Pittsburgh: Duquesne University Press, 1971.

Smith, Ronald Gregor. "Introduction" to Karl Jaspers, *The European Spirit.* London: SCM, 1948.

Sperna-Weiland, J. *Philosophy of Existence and Christianity: Kierkegaard's and Jaspers' Thoughts on Christianity.* Assen: Philosophia Religionis #3, 1951.

Thyssen, Johannes. "The Concept of 'Foundering' in Jaspers' Philosophy," in P. A. Schilpp, ed., *The Philosophy of Karl Jaspers*, pp. 297-336. New York: Tudor Publishing Co., 1957.

Tilliette, Xavier. *Karl Jaspers: Théorie de la Vérité, Metaphysique des Chiffres, Foi Philosophique.* Collection "Théologie" No. 44. Paris: Aubier, 1960.

Wahl, Jean. "Notes on Some Relations of Jaspers to Kierkegaard and Heidegger," in P. A. Schilpp, ed., *The Philosophy of Karl Jaspers*, pp. 393-406. New York: Tudor Publishing Co., 1957.

__________. *La Pensée de l'Existence.* Paris: Flammarion, 1951.

Wallraff, Charles. *Karl Jaspers: An Introduction to His Philosophy.* Princeton: Princeton University Press, 1970.

Welte, Bernard. *La Foi Philosophique Chez Jaspers et Saint Thomas d'Aquin.* Trans. by M. Zemb. Desclee-de Brower, 1958. Originally published as "Die philosophische Glaube bei Karl Jaspers und die Möglichkeit seiner Deutung durch die Thomistische Philosophie" in *Symposion 2* (1949), 1-190.

Wust, Peter. *Ungewissheit und Wagnis.* 4th ed. München: J. Kösel Verlag, 1946. Originally published in 1937.

3. Selected Literature on Religious Pluralism

Arapura, J. G. *Religion as Anxiety and Tranquility.* The Hague and Paris: Mouton, 1972.

Burch, George. *Alternative Goals in Religion.* Montreal: McGill-Queen's University Press, 1972.

Cameron, J. M. "Confusion Among Christians," *The New York Review of Books* (May 31, 1973), 19-22.

Christian, William. *Meaning and Truth in Religion.* Princeton: Princeton University Press, 1964.

__________. *Oppositions of Religious Doctrines.* London: Macmillan, 1972.

Davis, Charles. *Christ and the World Religions.* London: Hodder and Stoughton, 1970.

Del Vasto, Lanza. *Return to the Source.* Trans. by Jean Sidgwick. New York: Simon and Schuster, n.d.

Dunne, John. *The Way of All the Earth.* New York: Macmillan, 1972.

Eliade, Mircea and Joseph Kitagawa, eds. *The History of Religions: Essays in Methodology.* Chicago: The University of Chicago Press, 1959.

Friedmann, Maurice. "Touchstones of Reality," in Maurice Friedmann, T. Patrick Burke, and Samuel Laeuchli, *Searching in the Syntax of Things: Experiments in the Study of Religion*. Philadelphia: Fortress Press, 1972.

__________. *Touchstones of Reality*. New York: E. P. Dutton, 1974.

Hick, John. *God and the Universe of Faiths*. London: Macmillan, 1973.

__________. *Philosophy of Religion*. 2nd edition. Englewood Cliffs, New Jersey: Prentice Hall, 1973.

Hughes, Robert D. "Zen, Zurvan, and Zaehner: A memorial tribute to the late Spalding Professor of Eastern Religion and Ethics, Oxford," *Studies in Religion/Sciences Religieuses*, VI #2 (1976-1977), 139-148.

Kane, John. "Pluralism, Truth, and the Study of Religion," *Studies in Religion/Sciences Religieuses*, IV #3 (1974-1975), 158-168.

Mensching, Gustav. *Tolerance and Truth in Religion*. Trans. by H.-J. Klimkeit. University, Alabama: University of Alabama Press, 1971.

Merton, Thomas. *Mystics and Zen Masters*. New York: Dell, 1967.

Munz, Peter. *Problems of Religious Knowledge*. London: SCM, 1959.

Ogden, Schubert. "On Religion." Unpublished paper read for the seminar on "Religion, Myth, and Reason" at Dartmouth College, May 2-4, 1972.

Otto, Rudolf. *The Idea of the Holy*. Trans. by John W. Harvey. New York: Oxford University Press, 1958.

Radhakrishnan, S. *The Hindu View of Life*. New York: Macmillan, 3rd printing 1969.

Rahner, Karl. *Hearers of the Word*. Trans. by Michael Richards. New York: Herder and Herder, 1969.

Robinson, John-David, ed. *Word Out of Silence: A Symposium on World Spiritualities*. Special double issue of *Cross Currents*, XXIV #2-3 (Summer-Fall, 1974), 133-395.

Schleiermacher, Friedrich. *The Christian Faith*. Trans. by H. R. Mackintosh and J. S. Stewart. Edinburgh: T. & T. Clark, 1928.

__________. *On Religion*. Trans. by James Oman. New York: Harper & Row, 1958.

Smart, Ninian. "The Criteria of Truth as between Religions." Unpublished paper, n.d.

__________. *World Religions: A Dialogue.* Baltimore: Penguin, 1969.

Smith, Huston. "Introduction to the Revised Edition" of Frithjof Schuon, *The Transcendent Unity of Religions.* New York: Harper & Row, 1975.

Smith, Wilfred Cantwell. "Comparative Religion: Whither--and Why?" in Mircea Eliade and Joseph Kitagawa, eds., *The History of Religions*, pp. 31-58. Chicago: The University of Chicago Press, 1959.

__________. *The Meaning and End of Religion.* New York: New American Library, 1964.

__________. *Questions of Religious Truth.* New York: Scribner, 1967.

Thomas, Owen. "Introduction," to Owen Thomas, ed., *Attitudes Towards Other Religions.* New York: Harper & Row, 1969.

Tillich, Paul. *Christianity and the Encounter of World Religions.* New York: Columbia University Press, 1963.

Younger, Paul. *Introduction to Indian Religious Thought.* Philadelphia: The Westminster Press, 1972.

4. Other

Barth, Karl. *Protestant Thought: From Rousseau to Ritschl.* Trans. by Brian Cozens. New York: Simon and Schuster, 1969.

Bellah, Robert. *Beyond Belief: Essays on Religion in a Post-Traditional World.* New York: Harper & Row, 1970.

Berger, Peter. *A Rumor of Angels.* Garden City, New York: Doubleday, 1969.

Buber, Martin. "Eine Bekehrung," in *Begegnung: Autobiographische Fragmente.* Stuttgart: W. Kohlhammer Verlag, 1961.

Fackenheim, Emil. *God's Presence in History.* New York: New York University Press, 1970.

Flew, Anthony and Alasdair MacIntyre, eds. *New Essays in Philosophical Theology.* London: SCM, 1968.

Frank, Erich. *Philosophical Understanding and Religious Truth.* New York: Oxford University Press, 1966.

Grant, George. *Time As History.* Toronto: Canadian Broadcasting Company, 1969.

Hall, Roland. "Dialectic," *The Encyclopedia of Philosophy*, II, 385-389. New York: Macmillan and The Free Press, 1967.

Holmer, Paul. *C. S. Lewis: The Shape of His Faith and Thought*. New York: Harper & Row, 1976.

Lessing, G. E. *Lessing's Theological Writings*. Ed. by Owen Chadwick. London: Adam and Charles Black, 1956.

Lewis, C. S. *Surprised by Joy*. New York: Harcourt, Brace, and World, 1955.

Lynch, William. *Christ and Apollo: The Dimensions of the Literary Imagination*. New York: Mentor Omega, 1963.

__________. *Images of Faith*. Notre Dame: University of Notre Dame Press, 1973.

__________. *Images of Hope*. New York: Mentor Omega, 1966.

Murdoch, Iris. *The Sovereignty of Good*. London: Routledge and Kegan Paul, 1971.

Murti, T. R. V. *The Central Philosophy of Buddhism*. London: George Allen and Unwin, 1960.

Ogden, Schubert. *The Reality of God*. New York: Harper & Row, 1966.

Rahner, Karl. *Inquiries*. (n.p.) 1964.

Stringfellow, William. "Introduction," to Daniel Berrigan, *They Call Us Dead Men*. New York: Macmillan, 1966.

Von Hügel, Friedrich. *Essays and Addresses on the Philosophy of Religion: First Series*. London: J. M. Dent & Sons, 1921.

Wittgenstein, Ludwig. *Philosophical Investigations*. Oxford: Basil Blackwell, 1963.

INDEX

I. INDEX OF NAMES

II. SUBJECT INDEX